THE LEADERSHIP ADVANTAGE

JOEL D. SMITH

TABLE OF CONTENTS

Abstract

This manuscript charts a course through the dynamic realm of leadership, drawing parallels with the disciplined yet adaptive world of this officer/aviator. It presents a compelling narrative on the importance of readiness, calmness under pressure, and the power of reflective practice in navigating the complexities of leadership. Through engaging anecdotes and a professional, conversational tone, readers are invited to elevate their leadership approach, embodying the skills of a seasoned pilot to guide their teams through both clear skies and unforeseen turbulence.

- **Joel D. Smith**

Acknowledgements

Before I can even contemplate acknowledging anyone else, I must acknowledge my Lord and Savior, Jesus Christ. Without him, I would not have made it to this point in life. Next, I must acknowledge the man and woman who first loved me, my parents, Jobie and Roberta Smith. Mere words cannot convey the heartfelt thanks I feel for the path which you laid before me. Next, I have to acknowledge My bride, Katrina. Your faith, love, and support are the motivation I need to push forward daily. You bring peace to my world; you allow me to dream, focus, and create. To my children, through it all, you have made my journey as a father priceless, full of laughs and tears, and I wouldn't trade one moment of it. Quentin, Bryan, Natasha, Jeuan, Joel, and Katrese, I am so proud of each of you. To my heartbeats, my grandchildren.

Just as your parents dream big for you, know that your grandfather's dreams of your future are equally as big. You all are destined for greatness and my one prayer is you all hold onto God's unchanging hand and that you go make your dreams come true. To my sisters, Brenda and Midori, we may be all we have left but know that I couldn't love you more or be more thankful to have you in my life. To my brothers of Alpha Phi Alpha

Fraternity, Inc., thank you for your push to always move onward and upward.

To my wonderful extended family—aunts, nieces, nephews, in-laws, cousins—and to those I know better by nicknames than actual names, you know who you are! I am immensely grateful for your love and support.

To my chosen family, whom I affectionately call Momma, Poppa, Brother, and Sister, thank you for your invaluable support throughout this journey of life. You have stepped into roles that were much needed, and many of you continue to play these roles today.

To my teachers, coaches, and mentors, your relentless encouragement and push have helped me reach and exceed my limits. Your guidance has been pivotal in my growth from my athletic youth, through my military and pilot careers, to my current role as a coach. To my coach, Mr. Shaan Rais, and all of the staff at Omni Solutions, I thank you.

This new venture as a coach, while a fresh chapter, resonates deeply with my life's work and experiences. Coaching is a natural extension of my lifelong commitment to leadership and helping others. It's more than a profession—it's about the joy of seeing others achieve success and realizing their potential. Leadership is about people, it's about the unending space to soar. I cherish this opportunity to guide and inspire, just as I have been guided and inspired by each of you.

Foreword

Novice to Leader "Welcome to the Wolfpack Embracing the Leap: From Uncertainty to Leadership"

Hey there, my journey from a young man of African and Native American descent, raised in the shadows of a bustling army base within the vibrant yet challenging confines of a neighborhood affectionately known as "The Wood," to a seasoned leader, unfolds across a landscape marked by personal and societal transformation. Growing up in a community rich in diversity yet struggling against the backdrop of a nation grappling with its civil rights legacy, my story is a tapestry of simple truths and complex realities. As we proceed on this journey together, I will weave a few stories from my life into the total fabric of this body of work. I will also transition on occasion to my background in the aviation industry, both military and civilian. Remember, repetition aids learning, so some redundancy is intentionally placed throughout.

Guided by my parents, who believed in the power of resilience and the importance of adversity, I encountered a series of trials that carved my path to adulthood.

These experiences, daunting as they were, equipped me with a quartet of invaluable tools: Self/Team Development, Ethical Leadership, Communication, and, Trust (SECT)—my Core 4. Initially bewildering, these trials ultimately revealed their purpose, teaching me the essence of leadership: the courage to follow, the strength to lead, and the wisdom to know the difference, all while standing firm against the shadows of doubt and fear.

> *"The presence of fear does not mean you have no faith. Fear visits everyone. But make your fear a visitor and not a resident."*
>
> **Max Lucado.**

> *"Fear is only present in the absence of Faith."*
>
> **JDS**

It's within this framework that I was introduced to my initial assignment with the 82nd Aviation Brigade, 1/82nd Attack Battalion (Wolfpack), and my first hands-on experience with the AH-64 Apache Helicopter. This assignment not only marked my first stateside military role but also a pivotal chapter in my leadership development.

Here on the sprawling army installations known at the time as Ft. Bragg, (Ft. Liberty) the unit call sign, "Wolfpack," awakened the primal instinct within me— to strive, to thrive, not just for personal glory but for the survival and success of those fighting beside me. The ethos of the Wolfpack resonated deeply, echoing the intrinsic behaviors of wolves in the wild, where the success of the hunt relies not on the prowess of the individual, but on the seamless collaboration and strategic acumen of the entire pack.

Wolves, by nature, are quintessential symbols of teamwork and communication. In their world, each member of the pack plays a critical role in tracking, surrounding, and overcoming their prey. The alpha leads, setting the pace and direction, while others flank the sides, ready to support or redirect as the situation demands. This is not just a hunt; it's a choreographed dance of strength, agility, and intellect, where each step is purposeful and calculated for the collective benefit of the pack.

Drawing a parallel to my experiences with the 82nd Aviation Brigade, each mission we undertook was a testament to the power of collective effort and strategic execution. Like wolves on the hunt, we learned the importance of each role, the strength of silent communication through subtle cues and gestures, and the unyielding resolve to not only engage the mission but to adapt swiftly to the changing dynamics of the battlefield. The trust developed within our unit, much like that within a wolf pack, was not merely about reliance but about a deep-seated belief in the capabilities and the integrity of each member.

This pack mentality, instilled through our call sign, taught us that the strength of the group lies not only in physical capabilities but in the unity of purpose and the shared commitment to each other's success. Each operation was more than a mission; it was a collective endeavor to achieve what we set out to do, safeguarding not just individual lives but the integrity and success of the group as a whole.

In the wild, when wolves successfully take down their prey, it's a result of meticulous planning, flawless execution, and an unspoken understanding among the pack members of their roles and responsibilities. Similarly, in the military, especially within the esteemed ranks of the Wolfpack, every successful mission reinforced the tenet when we operate not as individuals but as a cohesive unit, attuned to one another's strengths and weaknesses, the potential for success exponentially increases.

Thus, the call sign "Wolfpack" was more than a moniker—it was a philosophy, a way of life that molded me into the leader I am today. It ingrained in me an unshakable belief in the power of unity and collective effort, virtues I carry into every arena of life, constantly reminded that like the wolves, we thrive best when we move not alone but as one formidable, indomitable pack.

This foreword sets the stage for a narrative rich with learning and insights, steeped in the realities of leadership, adversity, and the continuous pursuit of growth. Let's take this leap together, from uncertainty to leadership, and see where this journey takes us.

"For the strength of the Pack is the Wolf, and the strength of the Wolf is the Pack"

- Rudyard Kipling

WELCOME TO THE WOLF PACK
ELEVATE YOUR LEADERSHIP

Chapter 1

The Art Of Following Before Leading

My stubborn youth was marked by a blend of tenacity and resistance, a testament to the challenges of hardening and softening in equal measure. The quintessential lesson on my path to effective leadership was the realization that true leadership begins with the humility to follow. This cyclical lesson underscored a lifelong commitment to growth and self-discovery. The military, with its rigorous discipline and emphasis on teamwork, served as the launch point for transforming my identity and ego for a collective purpose. A purpose which was driven yet shaped me into a person possessing compassion and empathy. Now, when I talk about transforming my identity, I'm not referring to a total erasure of self-esteem or forgetting my roots and values. Instead, imagine gently placing your sense of self on a high shelf, out of immediate reach but still with in sight.

Before my journey in uniform ever began, the seeds of leadership and teamwork were being sown in a variety of playgrounds far removed from the structured discipline of military life. This might resonate with you if you've ever been part of a sports team, a club, or any group endeavor where the collective goal transcends individual ambition. My initiation into the dynamics of leading and following didn't start in training; it began as early as first grade, playing out across fields of competition and communal activities outside the classroom. From scouting adventures, baseball games, and bowling leagues to singing in the church youth choir and serving on the junior usher board, my early years were a vibrant tapestry of engagements. Each activity, each event, was a lesson in itself, teaching me the subtle art of leadership and the equally crucial skill of being a team player.

This wealth of experiences continued to expand through my undergraduate years, a period marked not just by academic learning but by profound personal growth within the brotherhood of Alpha Phi Alpha Fraternity, Inc. Here, amidst the camaraderie and challenges, I found numerous opportunities to lead, follow, and mentor. It was a time of personal growth against the backdrop of a nation in flux, still grappling with its history and striving toward racial equality.

Through these formative years, outside the conventional arenas of leadership training, I learned invaluable lessons about influence, responsibility, and the power of collective effort. These experiences laid the groundwork for the principles I would carry into my professional life, stressing the belief that leadership isn't confined to titles or roles but is woven through the cloth of daily interactions and commitments. My college days passed swiftly, and I soon found myself preparing for another journey, a journey which culminated with over 30 years of military service.

This portion of my journey, however, was not about glorifying the individual but about molding all who embarked upon it into a seamless unit, capable of achieving objectives far beyond the reach of any lone member. In the crisp air of my arrival day to basic training, clad in the uniform of a cadet, I encountered a profound realization—one which would shape my understanding of leadership in the most unexpected way. It wasn't about acquiring new skills or mastering drills that first challenged me; it was about letting go of something deeply personal: my identity, or more precisely, my ego. The idea of sidelining one's ego is, admittedly, a concept easier grasped in theory than in practice. Many believe they're ready to make this shift, yet find themselves unprepared or, at times, outright resistant when faced with the reality. It's a test of humility and adaptability, qualities as critical in the field as in the boardroom.

Lucky for us, our arrival was eagerly anticipated by a group of unique leaders, seasoned in the art of guiding novices through this very transformation. As our vehicle rolled to a halt at the in-processing center of the base, what awaited us was not so much a welcoming committee but the onset of a perfect storm, a force of nature resembling tornadic activity. Our Drill Sergeants—whom we grew to regard with a mix of respect and affection—were not just trainers but mentors, keen on helping us navigate the delicate balance between self and service.

Their expertise was not in breaking spirits but in forging leaders, skilled in the art of guiding without overshadowing, and instructing without dominating. Their arms were open, yes, but it was more in anticipation of briskly ushering us into our new reality. There would be no warm and loving embraces. Having grown up in a military family and enrolled in Army ROTC in college, I thought I had a leg up on understanding the dynamics of military life. I was wrong on so many different levels, nothing could have prepared me for the intensity of that first day—when it felt as though every person I met wanted a piece of my attention, all at the same time!

Among the pivotal moments was my encounter with Master Sergeant Phillips, whose unconventional welcome to basic training underscored the profound lesson of unity and submission to the greater good. I was tucked in the back of the van, surrounded by duffel bags, I soon developed an inkling that my choice of seat might have been less than ideal. This suspicion crystallized the moment the doors swung open to reveal Master

Sergeant Phillips standing like a gatekeeper between us and the world beyond. His presence filled the doorway, not so much blocking our exit as marking the threshold of a new reality.

In an instant, his reach extended over the seats towards me—Yes, me! It was a moment of direct contact, his hand firmly grasping my collar, not in anger but with the purposeful intent of a lesson waiting to be learned. The next thing I knew, I was being guided, somewhat abruptly, over the seats and out of the van. My landing was less than graceful, a swift introduction to the ground of the military base that would become my training ground in the weeks to come.

The "welcoming" that awaited me was not the kind of reception one might hope for, but it was very effective. There, on the ground, I was introduced to the ritual of "beating my face"—a euphemism in the military lexicon for performing push-ups... lots of push-ups. This exercise, a staple of military discipline, was my first real taste of the physical demands which would become a constant companion throughout my training.

In that moment, a flicker of doubt crossed my mind, replaying the decision to enlist like a questionable choice in a game of life. Lord, why had I so eagerly committed to this tumultuous journey? The paperwork which seemed so straightforward then, now felt like a pact teeming with challenges, revolving around a bunch of individuals who seemed to have never heard of using their inside voice as many parents have told their children.

In the early 80s, I stood about 6'4", my height might have been imposing had it not been for my slender frame of just 178 pounds, making me feel somewhat less formidable amidst the bustling environment of seasoned soldiers and urgent directives. It was a stark reminder of the physical and mental transformation awaiting me, a journey from the familiar to the wholly unknown, from civilian life to the disciplined structure of military training.

The experience, harrowing yet enlightening, imprinted on me the fundamental principles of leadership: active listening, authenticity, openmindedness, flexibility, humility, trust, clear communication, accountability, respect, relationship building, and continuous learning. I came to understand the animalistic tendencies I was developing; I had become a part of a pack.

We can draw invaluable leadership lessons from observing a pack of wolves. Consider their behavior during a trek: the pack positions the elderly and the sick at the front to set the pace. This ensures no member is left behind due to inability to keep up.

Just behind these vulnerable members are the strongest wolves, whose sole purpose is to guard and protect them. The center of the pack is shielded from both front and rear, creating a secure core. Further back, another group of strong wolves serves as the rear guard.

And who is at the very back? The leader. This wolf ensures the pack remains cohesive, guiding from behind, and ready to move in any direction to protect the group. This strategic position allows the leader to keep every member in sight, making swift decisions to safeguard the pack. This arrangement beautifully illustrates that true leadership isn't about taking the lead position—it's about nurturing and protecting the team, ensuring everyone progresses together safely along the journey. Let's not be confused, the leader is not always at the rear of the pack. However, this scenario presents a clear mindset of always being in the position to act/react.

Through humor and hardship, my military initiation coupled with the broader journey of life taught me the foundational importance of following as a precursor to leading. This early chapter of my life, woven with the threads of challenge, resilience, and discovery, laid the groundwork for a leadership philosophy rooted in trust, empathy, and the perpetual pursuit of growth.

I had completed college and all of my military training, and decided to head home for a bit before departing the country for my first duty assignment. Of course, that meant I had to go to church with my mother and there was going to be some form of small gathering at the house to enjoy a meal and fellowship. And if any of you were fortunate enough to know my mother, this meant over 100 people consisting of friends, family, and a number of people I did not know. As the evening was ending, my parents put me in the middle of those who remained gathered to pray for me and my journey. When it was all said and done, Mother pulled me off to the side and said one thing which has stuck with me to this day. She said, "Son, if you don't remember anything else, you remember this: You are your only limit. God hasn't placed any limits on you. So, don't you let a man put any on you either." Those five simple words have helped me to get through some tough times in some very challenging terrain under less-than-optimal conditions.

"There are two types of people in this world, limited and limitless, figure out which one you want to be."

- Derek Mason

Chapter 2

A Chat On Leadership's Real Deal

So, we're at this again, aren't we? Talking about leadership like it's some grand quest or epic journey. Well, in many ways, it is. But let's sit down by the firepit, grab a beverage, and chat about it like old friends. No jargon, no stiff collars—just you and me, figuring out this leadership gig together. Let's start with defining leadership. While many publications and dictionaries offer various definitions, however, I prefer to define it simply as relating, directing, coordinating a group, and providing guidance to progress to a common goal.

> *"If you don't have a seat at the table, then you're probably on the menu."*
>
> **-Unknown**

Never Stop Learning, Seriously.

Leadership? It's that never-ending class you didn't sign up for but got enrolled in any way. It's about learning from, well, literally everything. Think about it: every challenge missed, every target not quite reached at work—it's not just a setback; it's a rich, albeit tough, lesson in disguise. Analyzing what went wrong and strategizing how to move forward not only strengthens your problem-solving skills but also deepens your understanding of your team and the dynamics of your business.

Conversely, every success—like that presentation you nailed— serves as a confidence booster and adds a layer of expertise to your leadership skill set. It's not just about the applause; it's about understanding what worked and why, and how you can replicate this success in future endeavors.

The key to turning leadership into a lifelong class is maintaining an unyielding curiosity and openness to new ideas. The world around us is a vibrant ecosystem of information, constantly evolving and brimming with lessons to be learned. Staying tuned into changes, whether they're in technology, consumer behavior, or your own team's dynamics, ensures you're never falling behind but are always ready to adapt and evolve.

Engaging with peers, mentors, and even

competitors is another crucial aspect of this neverending education. Networking isn't just about building contacts; it's about exchanging ideas, challenges, and solutions. Every interaction has the potential to open doors to new perspectives and deepen your understanding of complex situations.

In leadership, there's never a true graduation day, and that's the beauty of it. The landscape is always changing, the lessons never cease, and the growth never stops. By embracing every day as an opportunity to learn something new, you ensure your leadership remains dynamic, informed, and impactful. Keep your eyes on the horizon, and your mind open, and remember— never stop learning, seriously.

Being Real is Your Superpower

Let's get real for a moment. Those moments when you feel most vulnerable. They're gold. Showing your human side, with flaws and all, actually draws people in. It's like saying, "Hey, I'm figuring this out too. Let's make sense of it together." Authenticity isn't just a buzzword; it's your secret weapon.

At the heart of impactful leadership lies a trait often celebrated yet challenging to consistently embody— authenticity. It's about being your true self, not just in solitude but in the full view of all, subordinates, peers, and superiors alike.

Authenticity is the art of being genuine, of ensuring that your actions and words mirror your true intentions and values. It's a trait that distinguishes great leaders, setting them apart not just for their strategic acumen but for their human touch.

Such leaders are marked by their vulnerability; they don't shy away from showing their own learning curves and moments of uncertainty. This openness fosters a culture where listening is valued as much as speaking. They engage with their team not from a distance but from within, genuinely interested in understanding the dreams, challenges, and ideas of those around them. This entails actually having a conversation from time to time to actively listen to your team. This active listening, the kind which seeks to understand before being understood, is fundamental. It's about seeking feedback not as a formality but as a crucial step in personal and organizational growth.

Being genuine means your honesty isn't just reserved for easy moments but is a constant in times of challenge and controversy. This integrity in leadership—being the same person in both quiet decisions and public announcements—cultivates a deep sense of trust. People follow not just the vision but the Leader themselves, believing in their consistency and dependability.

In a world that often rewards the loudest voice, authentic leaders prove that strength lies in transparency, in the courage to be oneself, and in the humility to listen. When leaders embody authenticity, they don't just build teams; they build trust, and with trust comes a foundation unshakable by the inevitable trials of any venture.

"Nothing is as fast as the speed of trust."

- Stephen Covey

It's All About the People.

If leadership were a movie, relationships would be the star. It's the little things—listening, really hearing what someone's saying, caring genuinely. It's about making everyone feel like they're part of this big, sometimes messy family. And guess what? That's where the magic happens.

Creating a sense of belonging is paramount, fostering an environment where everyone feels not just included but valued. This large, sometimes messy family atmosphere is where people feel safe to share ideas, express concerns, and contribute their unique perspectives. Think back through your life and the numerous relationships you've encountered. Play them over in your mind and you will realize just how much things play out like a movie. They weren't necessarily perfect events, but they provided multiple opportunities to reflect.

It's in this space the true magic of leadership is unleashed. Like the most memorable scenes in a film, these moments of connection, understanding, and mutual respect leave a lasting impact, resonating with everyone involved.

In the end, the measure of a leader's success is not just in the achievements and milestones but in the strength of the relationships forged in fire, sharpened in battle along the way. In the grand movie of leadership, it's clear: the people, the relationships, are not just the stars—they are the very soul of the story.

The Long Game: Leave Things Better Than You Found Them

Have you ever thought about what you'll leave behind? Not just the accomplishments, but the impact you've made on people, the planet— everything. It's about playing the long game, ensuring the world's a bit brighter, a tad kinder because you were here. A prime example is the effort worldwide (big in the United States) of small vendors selling Christmas trees. It seems like every year there are lots everywhere with trees available for purchase. Why, might you ask? It is because vendors and farmers continue to plant these trees after each harvest to ensure continual harvest for years to come.

The concept of the long game in leadership is similar to planting a forest in which future generations will find shade, thus ensuring we maintain a balance with nature—a commitment to leaving things better than we found them. It's a vision which transcends the immediate gratification of quick wins, focusing instead on the gradual but meaningful change we can instigate through our presence and actions. Does this sound simple yet grand to you? In actuality, it is but this can only be realized if it starts with the small choices we make every day.

Closing Thoughts: Just Between Us

Remember, leadership isn't about having all the answers. It's about asking the right questions and sometimes just being there, alongside your team, figuring it out step by step. Keep your heart in it, stay curious, and never forget the power of a good chat. Always keep in mind there exists a difference between leadership and likership. You will never be a friend to everyone and that's okay.

One of my former commanders said this when my family asked him during a unit Family Readiness Group meeting why I was always chosen to be the one on the first group out the door and in the last group to return. He simply replied like this, "My daddy always told me that when I have a good horse, you ride him. Joel is a thoroughbred who has my utmost trust to complete any task I give him well above standards or expectations." Needless to say, he didn't win any brownie points from my family on this particular evening.

Effective leadership? It's kind of like walking on a tight rope. On one side, you've got the need to be respected. Respect doesn't always come from making the crowd-pleasing decisions. Sometimes, you've got to call the shots that won't get you the most likes at home, in the boardroom, office, on campus, or on social media, if you know what I mean. It's about standing firm even when the applause is a bit...light.

Now, let's not forget the human side of things. It's about connecting, understanding, and yes, sometimes empathizing with your team. It's not all about cold, hard strategies and decisions; it's also about the people who help bring those plans to life. Another episode in my life involved a commander ensuring I made it home from overseas to pay my last respects to my grandfather. For those unfamiliar with how the military operates, this was not a standard practice as my grandfather was not a part of my immediate family (father, mother, sister, brother). His empathy shined through brightly as he knew what this man meant to me. He also recognized just how important it was to have his whole team ready and focused on the eminent task looming on the horizon. We would be soon asked by our nation to go to war.

So, here's the balancing act: meshing the human touch with the responsibility of steering the ship.

It's about earning your team's trust and respect, not just by what you decide but also by how you lead them through those decisions. And trust me, it's a delicate dance.

Leaders are the ones who find that sweet spot between being respected and making the tough calls needed for the organization to thrive. It's not about choosing one over the other; it's about weaving them together into the kind of leadership that moves people and the business forward.

Thanks for sitting down with me today. Here's to the crazy, beautiful leadership journey ahead—may it be filled with learning, authenticity, heartfelt connections, and, above all, a legacy that speaks volumes of the kindness and courage you shared along the way. Catch you on the flip side!

Chapter 3

Kicking Off: The Real Talk On Facing Challenges

Okay, let's dive a bit deeper into this adventure.

Because let's face it, leadership isn't always sunshine and rainbows. It's more like a rollercoaster ride in the dark—you never know when the next twist or turn is coming. But hey, that's part of the thrill, isn't it?

Riding the Waves of Adversity

Most of us have heard of Murphy's law, and I am certain most people have experienced it in some shape, form, or fashion during their day-to-day activities. You know those days when everything that can go wrong does? Yep, we've all been there. The real trick is not just to ride out the storm but to dance in the rain. You never realize how liberating just being in the rain without concerns about messing up your hair or having wet clothes or shoes can be. Adversity has this sneaky way of teaching us lessons we didn't think we needed or weren't necessarily looking for. It's about finding that silver lining, even if it's a bit water-soaked and tarnished. It's worth noting these moments of adversity aren't just hiccups or stumbling blocks in our journey; they are integral parts of the road itself. Each challenge, each setback has the potential to be a profound teacher. When everything appears to be falling apart, our true strength tends to show up—not just in how we manage to put things back together, but in how we manage to find growth in the process. These are invaluable lessons and must never be overlooked.

Adversity pushes us out of our comfort zones and forces us to innovate, to think on our feet, and to find resources we didn't know we had. It's during these times one's leadership is tested, and character...true character is formed. More often than not, the lessons learned from traversing these tough times provide the wisdom we need to handle future challenges with greater ease and confidence. The ability to maintain composure, to remain optimistic, and to lead others through uncertainty becomes a testament to our capability and resilience.

So, next time you find yourself in the midst of what seems like an unrelenting storm, remember this too is an opportunity to enhance your leadership repertoire. Embrace the chaos, learn from it, and let it remind you even the most tumultuous waves can lead to new shores of understanding and strength. Each wave ridden adds a layer of depth to your leadership abilities, turning potential adversity into a series of opportunities for personal and professional development.

EQ Over IQ: Why Your Heart Matters More Than Your Brain

I was often asked why I held such a burning desire to fly. My desire to fly came from a deeper place within me than mere curiosity. From a young age, the sky represented the ultimate canvas of freedom, a boundless expanse where dreams aren't just born, but are also realized. To fly is to embrace the liberty of the skies, to break free from the earthly ties that bind us, and to explore the realms of the almost impossible.

This longing to take to the skies was fueled by more than the allure of height and horizon; it was driven by a passion to join the birds, to get closer to God. Though each flight was not just a journey through the air or a test of skill, resilience, and courage, it was so much more for me as it represented peace and reflection for me. The Flight deck became my classroom and sanctuary, the aircraft, my instrument of learning and peace. With each flight, I was not just navigating through clouds but also through the complexities of my own capabilities and limits. Each flight also gave me points of clarity and, quite often, time to just simply think.

Thus, my desire to fly was more than a mere wish to soar; it was a yearning to grow, to lead, and to inspire. It was about pushing boundaries and expanding horizons, not just geographically but personally and professionally as well. Every takeoff was a new challenge, every landing a lesson learned, and every flight a reminder of the endless possibilities that lie just beyond the familiar.

Do you ever notice how the best leaders aren't always the smartest in the room? It is perfectly fine, and often beneficial, for leaders to not always be the smartest person in the room. They're the ones who truly get people. Just as flying embodies a physical escape into the skies, leading with the heart represents an emotional journey beyond the confines of logical constraints, diving into the realms of passion, empathy, and intuition.

When we consider why the heart might hold more sway than the brain in certain aspects of life, it's similar to understanding why a person might be driven to fly. The heart, like the desire to soar through the skies, is about following one's passions and deepest yearnings—it drives us to pursue paths that might seem illogical or risky to the calculating brain but feel profoundly right to our innermost selves. It pushes us towards authenticity and fulfillment, prioritizing what feels meaningful over what merely makes sense. Emotional intelligence—sounds fancy, but really, it's about understanding your feelings and those of others. It's laughing together, sharing a sigh, knowing when to push forward, and when to step back. By valuing and leveraging the collective intelligence of their team, leaders can drive their organization toward greater success, demonstrating effective leadership is more about asking the right questions than knowing everything. It's what makes leadership feel less like managing and more like connecting.

Joining Forces: Why Going Solo Is a No-Go

Leadership at its core isn't a solo sport; it's a team effort. It's about building bridges, not barriers. Think of it as being part of a band. Sure, you might have the microphone, but without your bandmates, it's just a solo act. And where's the fun in that? Everyone has their part to play; however, it is the leader who ensures everyone is playing at the same tempo, in the right keys to bring the beauty of the music together. The sweetest victories come from joint efforts— where everyone's tune adds to the harmony.

My time in the military more often than not revolved around collaboration and teamwork. The military operates around the clock, relying on the seamless integration of skills and efforts across various units and branches. This isn't just cooperation within a team; it's a broad-scale, interdependent system where every role, from the ground troops to the command officers, is pivotal. The military's effectiveness hinges on this orchestrated effort where coordination extends horizontally across peers, vertically across ranks, and diagonally across functions.

In situations where the mission's demands extended beyond our immediate capabilities, crossing lines into other services or even into collaborations with civilian sectors became essential. These moments underscored a vital leadership lesson: true success is a collective achievement, often requiring us to bridge gaps not only within our teams but across external entities and even industries.

This principle of extensive collaboration reflects a broader truth applicable to any leadership scenario, including in the business world. Today's leaders must be adept at navigating and networking beyond their immediate spheres, recognizing that the challenges of the modern world require joint efforts that span disciplines, industries, and even national borders.

As leaders, our task is to ensure each member of our team not only understands their role but feels valued for their contributions. We must cultivate an environment where diverse talents converge to create a cohesive whole, much like a band coming together to perform a captivating melody. The sweetest victories in leadership come from these collective efforts—where the harmony created by joining forces resonates far beyond the sum of individual contributions.

Planning for Tomorrow: Your Legacy Starts Today

Have you ever found yourself reflecting on the broader purpose of your daily grind? Ever asked,

"What's all this for?" Well, it's for those moments which take your breath away, the lives you touch, and the world you help shape for the better. Your legacy isn't just about what you achieve; it's about the impact you have. Little things make for big days. It's about planting trees under whose shade you may never sit but will offer comfort to future generations. It's in the compassionate words you share with a colleague, the courageous decisions you make when faced with adversity, and even in those quiet moments of support which might seem insignificant but mean the world to someone else. These aren't just fleeting moments; they are the building blocks of a lasting impact. And imagine, years from now, sitting with your grandchildren as their eyes widen, peaking with curiosity and awe as you share countless stories of your life. Tales of family traditions, your first big job, the hurdles of buying a home, or the joys and trials of raising a family. These stories are more than just personal memories; they are the pearls, diamonds if you will, of wisdom which will guide the next generation - your legacy passed on through words and experiences.

It's about understanding every day is a chance to add to this legacy. It's not just about grand achievements or high-profile successes; it's about the integrity, resilience, and compassion you embody. Each day provides new opportunities to influence, mentor, and contribute—not just to your immediate circle but to the broader community and society at large.

So, when you think about planning for tomorrow, remember your legacy starts today. It's built through every action, every interaction, and it's how you'll be remembered long after you're gone. Embrace this perspective, and let it guide you in making today meaningful— not just for you but for those who will follow in your footsteps.

> *"Believe in your dreams and they may come true;*
> *Believe in yourself and they will come true."*
>
> **- Unknown**

Wrapping It Up: From Me to You

So, as we wind down this chat, remember, leadership isn't about climbing to the top of the mountain alone; it's about bringing others along for the journey. It's about the scars, the laughs, the tears, and, most importantly, the growth. Brings to mind the Frankie Beverly and Maze song, "Joy and

Pain, It's Like Sunshine and Rain."

Keep it real, stay curious, and never forget, never give up: the essence of leadership is not just about where you're going, but who you become along the way. And hey, if you ever need a reminder, a pep talk, or just a moment to reflect—this conversation isn't going anywhere.

Here's to the wild, wonderful journey of leadership. May it be everything you hoped for and so much more. Until next time, keep leading with heart, and let's make this world a little better, together. Cheers to the ride of a lifetime!

Chapter 4

The Journey Continues: Embracing The Ups And Downs

Well, isn't this leadership journey a wild ride? Just when you think you've got it all figured out, life throws you a curveball. But hey, that's what keeps it interesting, right? Keep your eyes on the ball and follow it all the way through to the bat. You've got a hit, now let's keep this conversation going and dive into the art of bouncing back and keeping the spirit alive.

Embracing the Mess: Leadership Isn't Always Picture Perfect

Let's get one thing straight: leadership isn't about always being polished and perfect. It's about embracing the mess and the chaos, and finding your way through it. It's like being the captain of a ship in a storm; you might not control the weather, but you sure can steer the ship. Remember, it's okay to not have all the answers. The beauty is in the journey, in the learning, and in the growing.

I'll be the first to admit, there were plenty of times I found myself unable to see the forest for the trees, so caught up in the details that the bigger picture just evaded me. Take, for example, my training stints at the National Training Center in California—a true test of endurance and patience. Imagine the scorching desert in August, where the sun turns the world into an oven, especially when you're trying to get some sleep during the day in a tent which might as well be a sauna, with temperatures soaring past 110 degrees Fahrenheit. Lying in a puddle of your own sweat, rest isn't just elusive; it feels downright impossible.

You might wonder, "So what?" Well, here's the thing: all that discomfort had a purpose. It wasn't just about enduring the heat or managing without sleep. It was about preparation—getting ready for real-world missions in the Middle East where the environment was just as harsh, if not worse. The mantra "train as you fight" wasn't just a catchy phrase; it was our reality. We learned to embrace the suck, to accept and adapt to the discomfort because, in the grand scheme of things, these hardships were preparing us for the challenges ahead. The takeaways provided focus areas for improvements across the formation.

Despite the grueling conditions, the true beauty of this journey lay in its conclusion—returning home to the welcoming arms of family and friends. The hardships faced and the lessons learned all contributed to a greater appreciation of home, comfort, and community. Each challenging moment was a step on the path to becoming more resilient, not just as soldiers but as individuals.

The Heartbeat of a Team: Creating a Beat That Resonates

Building a team isn't just about gathering a bunch of talented folks. It's about creating a beat that everyone can groove to. It's the late-night pizza runs, the early-morning coffee and donut runs, the brainstorming sessions that turned into fullfledged disagreements or laughter fests. It's about finding the rhythm that makes everyone feel they're part of something bigger.

Indeed, there are times when a team member might seem out of sync with the rest, perhaps missing the beat when it comes to the group's rhythm. However, once they find their niche—their unique role, where they can truly shine—it's like striking the right melodic chord. Now, you can just sit back and enjoy the performance. This exemplifies the adage, "A team that plays together, stays together," highlighting the beauty of unity and synchronicity in team dynamics.

Consider the example of the Fab Five from Michigan. Yes, they faced a tough loss to Duke in the finals, but their journey to that point was nothing short of spectacular. This team, renowned for its cohesion and mutual understanding, showcased how deeply teammates can connect when they've grown together over time. They knew each other's strengths and weaknesses inside out, which made them formidable opponents on the basketball court.

Their time together had woven them into a tightknit fabric of shared goals and mutual support.

Let's apply this to the business world, when team members understand and complement each other's skills, the entire organization benefits. Just as in sports, in business, it's challenging to beat a team that's well-acquainted with its collective capabilities and limitations. Teams that have weathered various challenges and celebrated numerous victories together develop a deep-seated resilience and a nearly intuitive sense of collaboration.

In fostering such a team environment, it's crucial for leaders to encourage members to explore different roles and find where they can contribute most effectively. By nurturing an atmosphere where everyone can find and occupy their best niche, leaders set the stage for each member to perform optimally. When everyone is playing to their strengths, the team not only performs better but also enjoys a more harmonious and satisfying workplace experience.

Finding Your North Star: Guiding Principles in Leadership

In the maze of leadership, it is easy to get lost. This is why it is crucial to find your North Star—your guiding principles. This exploration deep dives into the core of what motivates and defines you as a leader. What foundational values do you adhere to, and what ideals do you stand for? These questions aren't mere reflections; they are the beacons that illuminate your path, especially through the most challenging times. Whether it's integrity, compassion, or courage, let these principles be your compass.

Imagine navigating the vastness of leadership as an explorer traverses' unknown territories, reminiscent of the days before navigation equipment existed on cars, ships, or planes. In this vast expanse, your North Star is the set of values you hold dear— integrity, compassion, resilience, or perhaps, a steadfast commitment to innovation and growth. These principles don't just offer direction; they embody the essence of your leadership identity, providing clarity and consistency in your decisions and actions. In layman's terms, they are the map which you use to navigate the business world.

This was the map which you possessed. It may not be perfect and a number of times you put handwritten notes and symbols on it yourself, but it provided the blueprint or foundation you needed if you ever veered off course. In the darkest of nights, when obstacles cloud your vision and the way forward seems fraught with uncertainty, your guiding principles shine the brightest. Like a lighthouse guiding ships tosafe harbor, or a rotating beacon guiding your eyes to the airport long before you see the runway, your core values lead you back to your true path, ensuring you remain true to your vision and purpose, regardless of the challenges that arise.

Let these principles serve as your moral compass, that reliable tool which doesn't just point you in the right direction but also offers reassurance that the path you're on aligns with your deepest convictions. Whether facing ethical dilemmas, strategic decisions, or interpersonal conflicts, always refer back to your guiding principles. They will help you navigate the complexities of leadership with integrity and purpose.

In essence, finding and adhering to your North Star is not just about setting a course; it's about defining who you are as a leader and what legacy you aim to leave behind. It's a commitment to leading not just with skill and acumen but with a heart and soul aligned with your deepest values.

Celebrating the Milestones: Because Every Step Counts.

Sometimes, in the hustle of chasing big goals, we forget to celebrate the little victories. But guess what? Every step forward is worth celebrating. Hit a small target?

Give yourself a pat on the back. Team member did something impressive?

Celebrate it. These moments of joy not only fuel our journey but remind us why we started in the first place.

Picture each milestone, no matter how big or small, as a beacon illuminating our path, reminding us of the progress we're making toward our grand vision, our end state. Celebrating these moments isn't just about acknowledging success; it's about reinforcing the behaviors and efforts which led to them. It's a practice which boosts morale, fosters a culture of appreciation, and encourages everyone to continue pushing forward, knowing their contributions are value d and recognized.

Moreover, the way we handle achievements and setbacks speaks volumes about our leadership. While successes should be celebrated openly, lending visibility to the achievements which collectively propel us forward, is equally important during the time required to handle corrections or address individual concerns with discretion and sensitivity. This balance ensures that while we openly celebrate our triumphs, we also maintain a supportive environment where feedback and growth are handled constructively and privately.

Cultivating a culture of acknowledgment for every step forward is vital not just for maintaining momentum but for reconnecting with the core reasons behind our collective efforts. Every major accomplishment is built from numerous smaller victories, each of which deserves its moment in the spotlight. This practice isn't merely about giving pats on the back; it's about infusing the team's journey with positive energy and a clear sense of purpose, keeping everyone aligned and motivated.

In the rigorous and high-stakes world of military aviation, this concept is exemplified by the journey pilots undertake to achieve the status of Pilot-inCommand. This significant milestone is not just a title—it symbolizes the pilot's transition from learner to leader, entrusted with the responsibility of not only flying but also maintaining and commanding a multi-million-dollar aircraft. The path to this point is marked by numerous smaller steps: each training session, each successful maneuver, and each increment of added responsibility.

For military pilots, reaching Pilot-in-Command is a profound honor and a moment of deep personal and professional pride. It's a testament to their dedication and skill, and it instills a sense of ownership which is highly cherished among aviators. Military pilots are often driven by a strong desire to be the best in their organization, and achieving this milestone is a recognition of their capability to lead, not just in the air but in all aspects of their roles as officers/aviators.

This drive for excellence and the acknowledgment of each milestone along the way is not unique to the military. In the business world, similar principles apply. When team members are recognized for their progress and achievements, they feel a greater sense of ownership and pride in their work. This fosters a motivated workplace where individuals are not only committed to their own roles but are also more inclined to contribute positively to the team's overall goals.

By embracing each small step as part of a larger journey, leaders can foster an environment where significant achievements are seen as collective victories. Whether in military aviation or in a corporate setting, the commitment to recognizing and celebrating every step ensures team members remain engaged and inspired throughout their careers.

Signing Off: But the Conversation Never Ends

As we wrap up this heart-to-heart, remember, the leadership journey does not have a finish line. It is an ongoing adventure, filled with highs and lows, triumphs and trials. But through it all, it's your passion, your resilience, and your willingness to make a difference that defines your leadership.

Keep your head up, stay true to yourself, and never stop striving to make the world a better place. And remember, this conversation, this journey of discovery, it's always here, ready to continue wherever you are.

So, until next time, keep leading with love, laughing often, and living fully. The best is yet to come, and I cannot wait to see where your leadership journey takes you. Onward and upward, my friend!

Chapter 5

The Adventure Awaits: Navigating New Horizons

"Before becoming a leader, success is about growing yourself. After becoming a leader, success is about growing others."

- Unknown

As we journey onward, remember, every new horizon is an opportunity for growth, an invitation to step into the unknown with courage and curiosity. Leadership is not just about leading others; it's about leading yourself through uncharted waters, discovering new depths to your abilities, and always aiming for the stars.

Remember, earlier we stated that leadership is cyclical and is truly never-ending. Here is to the leaders who dare to dream, to the trailblazers who paved the way, and to you—yes, you—for stepping up and taking on the challenge. The world needs more leaders like you, now more than ever.

The Strength in Vulnerability: A Leader's True Armor

What is one of the most powerful tools in your leadership arsenal? Vulnerability. Yes, you heard that right. It's not about armoring up against the world; it's about letting down your guard and showing your true self. It is in these moments of openness that we find the opportunities to build the strongest connections and find the most profound strength.

Being vulnerable is not about weakness; it's about courage—the courage to be real. It is the courage to be authentic, to acknowledge uncertainties, and to admit mistakes. Far from shrinking a leader's authority, this authenticity fosters a culture of trust and openness within teams and organizations. It encourages teams to engage in genuine dialogue, to share ideas without fear, and to contribute to the collective vision with honesty and integrity.

In moments of vulnerability, leaders do more than just share a piece of themselves; they open the door for deeper and lasting connections, for a shared sense of humanity which transcends the mere roles of leader and follower. It's within these spaces of openness that the strongest bonds are formed, and the most resilient teams are built. Teams rally not just behind a vision but behind a person who they see as approachable, relatable, and human.

There is something about saying the words, "I don't have the answer" or "I am weak in this area" which causes some individuals to cringe. As stated previously, true leaders/effective leaders know they do not have to be the smartest or strongest person in the room. The lesson I learned over the years and was reflective in the teams I was fortunate to lead, getting input from everyone increased development as everyone would inherently go back to self-study as we all wanted to be called upon at some point to provide the one piece of information which would drive the team home to victory.

The strength in vulnerability is, therefore, a leader's true armor. It protects not by shielding away the world but by engaging with it more openly and authentically. It is a reminder leadership is not about perfection but about the relentless pursuit of growth, both personal and collective. By embracing vulnerability, leaders show they are not infallible statues atop a pedestal but real, passionate individuals capable of effecting change and inspiring those around them.

These next few paragraphs were written while sitting in the lobby of the Moxy Hotel in Paris, France.

During one of the most challenging periods of my life, I encountered a situation which tested my resilience as a leader to its utmost. This experience centered around an inevitable part of life we all must face… death. It's a heavy topic, but one which profoundly shaped my understanding of leadership and duty. My story, though deeply personal, shares universal lessons on leadership and resilience. It unfolded during a critical period shortly after 9/11, when the echoes of national tragedy were still palpable, and the stakes of every military operation felt magnified.

While stationed overseas in Europe, my unit was engaged in a capstone exercise in a neighboring country, designed to culminate in a rigorous combined mission followed by a live-fire event. We had assigned crews for the mission, placed each crew on their assigned teams, and began mission planning. As one of the Standardization Instructor Pilots and a Master Gunner, my initial role was to participate directly in the night mission. However, plans shifted unexpectedly, pulling me from the unit planning process to the planning room to help orchestrate the live fire scenarios—a task which consumed the entire day and drew on my unique expertise.

The planning of the live fire event took all day to complete yet, we accomplished the task and were prepared to brief the command and all of the subordinate units of the plan. Upon completion, I returned to the unit operations center, only to be met with a significant and uncomfortable change in the atmosphere. The mission had moved forward without me, with aircraft assignments radically altered and already in motion. The individual who had replaced me, a fellow instructor, was someone whose path had closely mirrored mine, sharing not only professional spaces but personal milestones.

Later that night, the stark news arrived. The instructor who took my place perished in the very aircraft I was initially slated to fly. This loss was harrowing, compounded by eerie coincidences which made the event feel intensely personal:

1. We arrived in the country just four days apart.

2. We both shared a faith and love for God.

3. We celebrated the same wedding anniversary— a date now marred by tragedy for his wife, who learned of her husband's death that very morning.

In the wake of this loss, I grappled with overwhelming grief and guilt, questioning my role and responsibility as a leader who was not in command yet felt every inch of the burden of command. The convergence of our shared lives and the sudden, jarring end to his brought me to the brink of resigning my commission, stepping away from a career of 14 years which had defined much of my adult life.

It was a mentor's timely intervention which guided me through this storm. Sitting in my office, he urged me to consider the wider impact of my potential decisions. He reminded me to look into the eyes of those I was senior to, who sought guidance and stability in my actions. This conversation, along with heartfelt discussions with the commander, fellow service members, the fallen instructor's family, and in solitude with my faith, slowly steered me back towards a path of duty and leadership.

These dialogues, painful yet stimulating, were transformative. I came to understand better my role as a leader was not diminished by the tragedy but was instead crucial to the healing and forward movement of the team. I returned to my duties with a renewed sense of purpose, honoring my fallen comrade through continued service and dedication to training the next generation of warriors.

"Don't let yesterday take up too much of today."

- Will Rogers

Throughout the rest of my military career and into retirement, I have carried this story as a testament to the enduring power of resilient leadership. It serves as a reminder we lead not just in moments of triumph but perhaps more importantly, through times of great adversity.

This journey through loss and recovery underscored the essence of true leadership: the ability to navigate through personal and collective pain, to find strength in vulnerability, and to emerge with a deeper commitment to the values we hold dear. It's a narrative I share to illuminate the path for others, proving even in the darkest times, leadership can be a beacon of hope and transformation.

Chapter 6

Turning Loss Into Victory: Lessons Forged In The Fire Of Tragedy

Introduction: Embracing the Storm

Every leader's journey is marked by trials and tribulations, some so severe they threaten to break our spirit and resolve. The story I just shared reflects one of the darkest periods in my own life, a time of deep personal and professional turmoil.

It's in these crucibles of adversity that the true essence of leadership is not merely tested; it is refined and forged in fire.

Leadership in the face of such adversity isn't merely about enduring; it's about extracting wisdom from the pain, growing from the experience, and emerging stronger. This process of transformation is intensely challenging. It involves confronting the rawest parts of ourselves and our circumstances, questioning and redefining what we believe, and ultimately using that newfound strength to propel ourselves forward with renewed vigor and resolve.

The art of transforming loss into victory is a complex dance of accepting the pain of the setback while refusing to be defined by it. It's about understanding these moments, as harrowing as they are, holding invaluable lessons which are integral to our growth. This isn't about denying the hurt but about facing it head-on, learning its contours, and turning it into a catalyst for profound personal and leadership development.

In leadership, as in life, the storms we face can tear down our world or, conversely, clear a path for new growth and opportunities. The choice lies in how we respond to them. As leaders, we have the responsibility not only to manage our own responses but also to guide those who look to us for direction and hope through their own challenges.

Through embracing these storms, we discover not only the depths of our own strength but also the essential qualities which make us effective and compassionate leaders. It is here, in these moments of tested resolve, true leaders are made—tempered and tutored by the trials they have overcome.

Resilience: The Backbone of Leadership, Learning to Stand Again

Resilience is the ability to recover from setbacks and adapt to change. In the business world, this translates to bouncing back from market downturns, technological disruptions, or internal crises. Tragedy and loss are harsh teachers, but the lessons they impart are invaluable. They teach us resilience—the kind which comes from facing your darkest moments and choosing to light a candle rather than curse the darkness. This resilience becomes a cornerstone of effective leadership, showing us our capacity to endure and overcome is far greater than we ever imagined.

Allow me to put another personal moment to paper. My unit was preparing to deploy into a hostile environment. As showtime was around 4:00 am, I attempted to say so long to the kids the night before. This did not happen as everyone wanted to see Daddy off. Little did I know I was going to face one of those dark moments. As everyone was getting their goodbye hugs in, my youngest daughter approached me last and stated something which struck me square in the chest. She stated, "Daddy, my birthday must not mean anything to you as you are never here for it." Talk about being thrown for a loop. As I picked up my baby girl to say so long, I kissed her on the cheek and said I apologize.

During the next 36 hours of traveling, I had time to reflect, and she was right. My seven-year-old was absolutely right. She is an August child, and every year like clockwork, I found myself deployed either to the field, school, or hostile environment. Her special day always took me somewhere other than home. This made me look at my other children and think of their birthdays and all of the special events I had missed. I had to light a candle of my own to navigate the often-conflicting life of a military officer with that of being a loving father. Surprisingly enough, the following August, I was enrolled yet again into a military course. However, this time I flew her to me, and we had cake and ice cream in my hotel room once I got out of class. Though the act itself was small, it was necessary for my youngest as she lit the candle to shine the way through the darkness.

In the corporate world, resilience is about much more than recovery; it's about proactive adaptation and strategic foresight. When the market takes a downturn, resilient leaders look beyond immediate losses to the potential for future gains. They see these challenges as opportunities to innovate and reinvent their strategies. Similarly, when new technologies disrupt established ways of working, resilient leaders and companies are those who don't merely adjust but embrace these changes, leveraging new tools to enhance their competitive edge.

A great example of this comes from Kenneth Chenault, former CEO of American Express, who exemplified resilience. Under his leadership during the fallout from the 9/11 attacks and the 2008 financial crisis, Chenault steered American Express through significant challenges by focusing on innovation and customer service, ultimately returning the company to strength.

While no one wishes for hardship, there's an undeniable truth tragedy and loss are profound educators. They strip away the unnecessary, exposing the core of our values and testing the strength of our convictions. These moments demand that we either succumb to despair or rise with a renewed sense of purpose. Choosing to 'light a candle'—to find a path forward in the darkness— not only illuminates our own way but also guides those who depend on our leadership.

This kind of resilience does more than showcase our ability to endure; it reveals our capacity to transform challenges into catalysts for growth. It demonstrates our potential to lead effectively through adversity is far greater than we might have previously imagined. For a leader, embodying resilience can inspire a whole organization, fostering a culture where challenges are met with courage and creativity rather than fear and frustration.

It cultivates an environment where setbacks are seen not as endpoints but as bends in the road, inviting innovative thinking and renewed efforts. Resilient leaders not only recover from falls—they climb higher, encouraged by the knowledge every challenge overcome is another proof of their capacity to lead under any circumstances.

"Obstacles are those frightful things you see When you take your eyes off your goal."

- Henry Ford

Empathy: Connecting Through Shared Struggles, Leadership That Understands

Trials and tribulations teach us empathy. Having navigated through the tumultuous waters of loss ourselves, we gain a deeper understanding of the struggles of those we lead. This empathy enables us to connect with our team on a more meaningful level, to lead not just with directives, but with compassion and understanding.

Empathy in leadership means truly understanding and sharing the feelings of others. This trait is crucial, especially in times of collective hardship. Ursula Burns, the first African American woman to lead a Fortune 500 company as CEO of Xerox, is renowned for her empathetic leadership style. She focused on inclusivity and diversity, recognizing a supportive culture leads to a more committed and productive workforce. From the ashes of tragedy, leaders can also learn adaptability. Often, our greatest plans are upended not by minor obstacles but by significant, unforeseen challenges.

Remember Murphy's Law, yes, it still has a vote and will cast it at the most in opportune times. Learning to pivot, to find new paths through the wilderness of the unexpected, is a skill developed and finely honed during the hardest of times. It's about finding victory in the flexibility of our strategies and the unyielding spirit of our pursuit.

Perhaps most importantly, turning loss into victory is about finding meaning in the struggle. It's about using our experiences of defeat and grief as a beacon for others, showing it's possible to emerge from the depths of despair with new wisdom and a renewed purpose. Our trials, when shared, can inspire resilience, hope, and action in others, multiplying our impact far beyond our individual achievements.

> *"See, to live is to suffer, to survive, well, is to find meaning in the suffering."*
>
> **DMX**

In crafting a leadership narrative which includes the transformation of loss into a victory, we are reminded leadership is as much about traversing through storms as it is about moving through the calm skies and waters. The lessons learned from facing adversity not only shape us into more resilient, empathetic, and adaptable leaders but also teach us the profound value of perseverance and the power of HOPE. This chapter of our journey underscores the belief even in the aftermath of tragedy, small or big, there lies potential for monumental victory—a victory not just for ourselves but for all those we desire to inspire and lead.

> *"If you're going through hell, keep going."*
>
> **Winston Churchill**

Adaptability: Pivoting with Purpose, When Plans Change, Leaders Evolve

In the ever-shifting landscape of business and leadership, adaptability isn't just a skill—it's a crucial survival trait. It involves not merely reacting to changes but proactively adjusting strategies to harness the potential of new conditions. This dynamic approach enables leaders to not only withstand unforeseen challenges but to leverage them for enhanced performance and innovation. Adaptability is about adjusting strategies in response to unforeseen challenges.

A prime example of this principle in action is seen in the career of Robert F. Smith, the founder of Vista Equity Partners. Smith's focus on technology and software sectors—industries known for their resilience and rapid growth—exemplifies strategic adaptability. His ability to steer the firm's investment strategies towards these high-growth areas has allowed Vista Equity Partners to thrive, even during periods of economic downturns.

The firm's success under Smith's leadership showcases how adaptability goes beyond mere survival; it involves identifying and capitalizing on opportunities others might overlook. By focusing on sectors that are inherently less susceptible to market fluctuations, Smith not only safeguarded his firm but also positioned it for exponential growth.

Embracing adaptability means seeing every change as an opportunity to improve and refine your approach. It's about staying informed on industry trends, anticipating market shifts, and being prepared to pivot your strategies at a moment's notice. This readiness isn't just about having a backup plan; it's about integrating flexibility into your core business model and leadership style. This sounds a lot like playing a game of chess or being a military commander employing tactics and strategies to your long-term goals and objectives.

For leaders, this means fostering a culture where change is not feared but welcomed as part of the evolutionary process. It's about encouraging teams to be agile, to experiment, and to learn from each iteration. This culture of adaptability ensures an organization is not rigidly tied to one path but is continually evolving and improving.

Expanding beyond the business sector, the principle of adaptability is relevant to various aspects of leadership. Whether managing a small team or leading a large corporation, the ability to pivot with purpose and re-align resources according to shifting needs is essential for sustained success and relevance.

Meaning: The Beacon of Hope, Inspiring a Future Beyond the Crisis

Finding meaning in adversity involves using personal and collective trials as a source of inspiration for others. Oprah Winfrey's journey from poverty and hardship to becoming a media mogul and philanthropist shows how personal challenges can be transformed into platforms for broader social impact. Her story encouraged and continues to encourage others to find strength and meaning in their struggles and to see adversity as a catalyst for growth and change.

Legacy of Leadership

The journey from loss to victory in leadership transcends beyond mere moments of triumph; as it is a relentless pursuit of personal growth, continual learning, and profound inspiration. It's about the transformation which occurs when leaders not only face their challenges but also embrace them, using their experiences as a beacon for others. This process doesn't just build a personal legacy; it has the power to elevate entire communities and industries, catalyzing widespread change and development.

Leaders who fully embrace their experiences, particularly the challenging ones, and channel these into lessons for others, do much more than create personal legacies; they lift entire communities and sectors. This process involves more than resilience; it requires a deep-seated empathy for others' struggles, an adaptability to continually shifting circumstances, and a never-ending search for deeper meaning in all endeavors.

Reflecting on the journeys of notable African American leaders, we gain invaluable insights into how challenges can be transformed into powerful narratives of success. These leaders demonstrate time and again how resilience can propel us forward, how empathy enriches our interactions, and how adaptability ensures our relevance in an ever-changing world. Their lives and careers offer blueprints for harnessing personal hardships and societal obstacles as catalysts for substantial leadership growth.

The lessons gleaned from such trailblazers show us leadership is indeed a visionary act, one which looks beyond the present turmoil to a future ripe with potential. By adopting these principles— resilience, empathy, adaptability, and a pursuit of meaning— leaders today can prepare not only themselves but also their followers to face future challenges with confidence and a robust vision for success.

As leaders, your task is to forge paths that others can follow, to light the way through our actions and decisions, and to inspire future generations to carry the torch forward. This is the essence of a true legacy—a lasting impact which nurtures and cultivates potential in others, turning individual achievements into communal victories and personal resilience into collective strength.

Thus, the legacy of leadership is crafted through each decision, each challenge faced, and each lesson shared. It is a collage made up of countless individual pieces, each colored by our experiences and shaped by our responses. As we continue to lead, let us do so with the knowledge our actions today write the history of tomorrow, inspiring others to rise, learn, and lead.

Laughing Through the Chaos: The Lightness in Leadership

Let us not forget to laugh, especially at ourselves. Leadership comes with its fair share of bumps and bruises, and sometimes, the only thing you can do is laugh. It's this lightness, this ability to find humor even amid chaos, which keeps us grounded. A good laugh can be the best remedy, a way to lift spirits and remind us that, at the end of the day, we are all human. Embracing a sense of humor can transform the workplace atmosphere, making it more conducive to creativity, collaboration, and resilience.

The comedian Katt Williams said during one of his tours, "You should get at least seven chuckles a day." I do not believe he was talking about a simple giggle; I believe he meant the kind of laughter to bring tears to your eyes. You will feel so much better after it is over, even if your stomach hurts a little. True enough, laughter at the moment may not necessarily resolve the problem, it may however provide a unique opportunity to view the issue through another lens. This may in fact be just what was needed, no matter how unorthodox the means of getting there may seem.

Laughter is a universal language able to bridge diverse groups and soften the rough edges of a highpressure environment. By fostering a culture where laughter is a common sound, leaders can enhance team cohesion and forge bonds which might not otherwise form in a strictly formal work setting. This sense of camaraderie is crucial for building a team able to rely on each other and work effectively together, especially when facing challenges.

Moreover, strategic use of humor can be an effective way to boost morale and increase productivity. When employees are in good spirits, they are likely to be more engaged with their work and more productive. Recognizing the appropriate moments to add lightness can revitalize a weary team, help put setbacks into perspective, and renew energy for the tasks at hand.

Leaders who practice and propagate a balanced approach to work, where seriousness about goals coexists with light-hearted interactions, create a more enjoyable and sustainable working environment. This balance helps prevent burnout and keeps the team motivated over the long haul. It also shows the leader values not only the end results but the process and well-being of the team.

Integrating humor and lightness into leadership is not about diminishing the seriousness of the job. Instead, it's about enhancing the leader's ability to deal with adversity, connect with their team, and create a positive work environment. As we navigate the complexities of leadership, let us remember this, sometimes laughing through the chaos can be the most rational act of all. It's these moments of shared laughter and lightness which can make the journey worthwhile, and lead to a team which is not only successful but also happy and deeply connected.

Crafting Your Story: Every Leader Has One to Tell

Your leadership journey is uniquely yours, a story only you can tell. And what a story it is—filled with plot twists, victories, challenges, and lessons learned. Sharing your story isn't just about recounting your successes; it's about the wisdom gained along the way, the moments of insight, and the experiences that have shaped you.

Talking about the times you stumbled isn't just airing out dirty laundry. It's actually pretty powerful. It shows others it's okay to take risks and make mistakes. Basically, it's like saying, "Hey, I messed up too, but look where I am now." It's about stepping into the light and ditching the cloak of invisibility. Your story has this incredible potential to motivate, to teach, and to connect with others on a real level.

So, don't hold back or think your story isn't worth sharing. Each one of us has something valuable to contribute, lessons that can light the way for someone else. Be the one to break the ice, come out of the shadows, and no longer subscribe to obscurity. Your story has the power to inspire, to teach, and to connect. So don't be shy—share it with the world as only you can do. After all, your leadership tale is not just about where you've been but also about where others might go because of what you've shared.

The Ripple Effect: Making Waves with Your Leadership

Never underestimate the impact you can have. I was reflecting on my youth and a time as a kid, whenever we would go out to the lake in Ft. Campbell, KY, it was inevitable rocks were going to be thrown in an attempt to skip them across the water. It dawned on me that just like a pebble tossed into a body of water, our leadership can create ripples which extend far beyond our immediate reach. It's about the lives you touch, the change you inspire, and the legacy you leave behind. Leadership is not just about making waves; it's about setting in motion a tide of positive change which can transform the world.

I believe this is what motivates individuals to become teachers, instructors, or coaches. It is the burning desire to impart knowledge, change a mindset, and help individuals and teams achieve all they can. What I find humorous is those who say I could never be a teacher, when becoming a leader inherently makes you just that...a teacher/instructor/coach. In a lifetime, it is impossible to never delve into the role of leadership. Face it, we are always destined to lead in some capacity. The sooner we own it, the easier it will be to take those first steps.

Until Next Time: Keep Shining, Keep Leading

As we part ways for now, take a moment to reflect on the journey so far and the paths yet to be explored. Leadership is an ever-evolving adventure, a continuous quest for growth, understanding, and connection. Your leadership light is needed now more than ever in a world craving guidance, hope, and inspiration.

So, keep shining, keep pushing boundaries, and keep leading with heart. The world is a better place with you at the helm, guiding us towards a brighter future.

And remember, this isn't goodbye; it's just a pause in the conversation. There's always more to explore, more to learn, and more to share. I'll be here, cheering you on, ready to dive back into the adventure wherever you are.

Here's to the endless journey of leadership, to the stories yet to be written, and to the incredible impact you're destined to make. Catch you on the next wave, leader. The adventure continues, and it's going to be epic!

Chapter 7

The Adventure Deepens: Turning Obstacles Into Opportunities

Alright, let's keep rolling with this. Leadership isn't just about navigating through the clear skies; it's also about turning those inevitable storms into opportunities for growth. Imagine each obstacle not as a roadblock but as a stepping stone toward becoming a more resilient, empathetic, and insightful leader. Sounds like a plan, doesn't it?

Laughing in the Face of Challenges

Are we talking about laughing again? why yes, we are. Why is this coming up again, you may ask? I am trying to convey the significance of never allowing circumstances to pull you down even when they seem insurmountable. Have you ever hit a challenge so massive all you could do was crack up? Picture a Kevin Hart-style reaction after one of his epic stand-up bits.

There's something super powerful about spotting the humor in a total mess. There are times when he is so into the tale, he has no choice but to laugh at himself, preventing him from getting the rest of the story out at that specific moment. When he finally finishes the tale, you laugh even harder. It kind of puts things into perspective, doesn't it? Like, you're throwing your head back and saying, "Alright, universe, you've thrown me a curveball, but just wait and see what I do next."

This isn't just about making light of the situation; it's a strategy which can really pull your team together. It shows everyone it's totally fine to find a slice of happiness, even when things look grim.

It's a reminder we're just in a tough spot for now, and like all tough spots, it's going to change. I had a pastor say once, "Life is full of seasons. In time, the season you find yourself in will change, just hold on a little bit longer."

Take, for instance, Maya Angelou. She faced unimaginable challenges throughout her life, from racial discrimination to personal traumas, yet she never lost her incredible sense of humor and wit. Or consider Barack Obama, who, amidst the intense pressures and criticisms during his presidency, often used humor to defuse tension and connect with people on a human level. These figures didn't just endure; they laughed in the face of challenges, showing us all how resilience and joy can coexist.

The Secret Ingredient: Empathy

If there's one thing which can truly transform your leadership style, it's empathy. Putting yourself in others' shoes, and understanding their struggles, hopes, and dreams—changes the game. It's not just about leading; it's about connecting on a human level. This isn't some fluffy concept; it's the glue which holds teams together, especially when the going gets tough.

Flipping the coin over, an overemphasis on empathy, without balancing it with practical decision-making, can sometimes lead to challenges in leadership. While empathy encourages understanding and connection, it must be complemented by the ability to make tough decisions when necessary. Leadership isn't only about connecting on a human level; it's also about guiding a team towards achieving its objectives.

This requires a blend of empathy and decisiveness, as being too absorbed in the emotional aspects can hinder the ability to act with the necessary objectivity and firmness.

The art of leadership involves balancing empathy with a clear vision and the courage to make difficult choices, ensuring empathy enriches rather than impedes the decision-making process. Leading isn't just about being on the same wavelength with your team; it's also about steering the ship, even when the seas get choppy. Balancing that emotional insight with a dash of decisiveness is the real secret sauce to leadership. It's what keeps the team tight and on track, no matter what.

Mistakes: The Ultimate Teachers

Alright, let's dive into a topic we usually avoid like the last slice of pizza nobody wants to admit they are eyeing—mistakes. Yeah, those cringe-worthy moments when things go south, and you wish you could hit a giant "undo" button. But plot twist: these blunders, as much as they sting, are pretty much the best mentors you ever wanted. Each slipup hands you a winning lottery ticket to learning, sharpening your skills, and maybe most importantly, setting a chill vibe for your team letting them know it's cool to drop the ball sometimes.

What really counts isn't the stumble itself but the colossal comeback. It's about picking yourself up, dusting off, and having that lightbulb moment where everything clicks, and you suddenly know so much more than you did. So, the next time you face plant spectacularly, pause for a beat. Do a little introspection, maybe even embrace the strawberry on your chin, and then zoom forward armed with insights and the fire to get it right, or maybe wrong again, but better each time.

Adding a bit more to the mix, consider the way great innovators talk about their failures. Steve Jobs, for instance, was booted from his own company, only to learn, grow, and eventually come back to lead Apple to unimagined success. Or Oprah Winfrey, who faced numerous setbacks in her early career but used each one as a stepping stone to become a media mogul. Their journeys remind us that the path to greatness is paved with not-so-great moments, and that's perfectly okay.

Staying True to Your Course

In this maelstrom of leadership, it's easy to lose sight of your direction. That's why it's crucial to check in with yourself regularly. Are you staying true to your values, your vision, your mission, your north star? This isn't about being stubborn but about being grounded in what matters most to you and your team. It's your authenticity which will inspire others to follow, even when the path seems uncertain. Being authentic, committed, and consistent leads to a key tool in every leader's tool kit…Trust.

General Colon Powell stated, "Leadership ultimately comes down to creating conditions of trust within an organization. Good leaders are people who are trusted by their followers. Effective leaders take organizations past the level that the science of management says is possible."

Never The End: Just a New Beginning

And here we are, at what seems like the end of our chat, but really, it's just another beginning. Leadership is an endless journey of discovery, growth, and connection. It's about embracing every moment, learning from every experience, and always striving to be a little better than you were yesterday.

Keep your heart open, your mind curious, and your spirit adventurous. Remember, the impact you make isn't just about the goals you achieve but the lives you touch along the way.

So, as we part ways (for now), take a deep breath, smile, and step forward with confidence. The world is waiting for your unique brand of leadership. Go out there and make a difference, one step, one laugh, one act of kindness at a time.

Until our paths cross again, keep shining, keep leading, and remember—this is just the beginning of something extraordinary. Here's to the endless adventure of leadership, to the stories we'll tell, and to the incredible journey that lies ahead. Onward, to the next chapter!

Chapter 8

The Path Unfolds: Building Your Legacy One Step At A Time

Well, here we are again, sitting by the firepit talking about this journey together, figuring out leadership and each necessary step we will encounter along the way. It's not just about the destination but the footprints we leave behind. Let's keep this journey going, shall we? After all, every conversation, every shared moment, adds up to the legacy we're building.

Crafting Moments That Matter

Think about it: leadership isn't just a list of achievements; it's the collection of moments that matter, the moments which really stick with you. It's those times when you choose to stand up for what's right. Or those times you actually listened, like really listened, to someone who just needed a bit of your time and attention. To lend an ear when someone needed to be heard, or to inspire your team to push a little harder, not because they had to, but because they wanted to. It's about more than hearing words; it's about understanding context, emotions, and underlying messages. These are the bits and pieces where your true impact as a leader starts to take form, in the quiet corners of day-today life, shaping a legacy that's felt more than it's seen.

Consider the power of standing up for what's right, especially when it's easier not to. Leadership involves making decisions which adhere to ethical principles, even under pressure. These instances might not make headlines but are often the moments which earn a leader genuine respect and loyalty from their team.

Moreover, inspiring your team to go above and beyond is a hallmark of effective leadership. It's one thing to push a team because you have

authority; it's another to motivate them so they are driven by their own enthusiasm and commitment. These moments, when you encourage your team not just to meet expectations but to exceed them out of a genuine desire to achieve, are the building blocks of a deeply motivated and cohesive team.

Much of a leader's real impact is shaped away from the spotlight, in the quiet corners of day-to-day interactions. It is here, in the daily grind, that the foundation of trust and respect is laid. Each small decision, each moment of kindness, and each instance of unwavering support combine to craft a legacy which is felt deeply by those who are experiencing it firsthand.

When reflecting on leaders who have left an indelible mark on their fields, it is rarely their public accolades which stand out. Instead, it's how they handled crises with composure, led with unwavering passion, and made every team member feel seen and valued. These leaders are remembered not just for what they accomplished, but for how they made people feel, how they enhanced lives, and how they quietly shaped the world around them.

In essence, the true measure of leadership is not quantified by achievements which can be listed on a resume but by the meaningful moments which resonate with others. These moments of integrity, empathy, motivation, and genuine interaction define what leadership truly means and form the legacy that endures well beyond a leader's tenure. As leaders, our challenge and opportunity lie in recognizing and nurturing these moments, for they are where our deepest impact is made.

Staying Humble, Staying Hungry

In the dynamic world of leadership, striking the right balance between humility and ambition is not just beneficial—it's essential. This balance keeps us anchored yet propels us forward, ensuring we navigate our roles with both wisdom and enthusiasm. As we journey through leadership, it's crucial to stay humble and hungry.

Being humble in leadership means recognizing no matter the heights we reach, there's always more to learn and space to improve. This humility prevents arrogance and complacency, creating a culture where continuous learning is valued and encouraged. It encourages leaders to remain open to feedback, to question their own assumptions, and to continually assess their approaches. This openness not only enhances personal growth but also sets a powerful example for others, promoting a team environment where curiosity and personal development are integral to the culture.

Conversely, staying hungry for new challenges and experiences drives innovation and prevents stagnation. It's about constantly seeking new goals, dreaming bigger, and pursuing new adventures that push the boundaries of what's possible. This relentless pursuit keeps a leader and their organization dynamically evolving, adapting to new markets, technologies, and opportunities. It ensures a leader's journey is never static but is an ongoing adventure marked by perpetual growth and exciting ventures.

The interplay between humility and hunger is what keeps a leader grounded yet aspiring for more. Humility reminds us to be grateful for our achievements and the people who have supported us along the way. It teaches us to value the journey itself and not just the destination.

Meanwhile, a healthy appetite for achievement fuels our drive to venture beyond our comfort zones and explore uncharted territories. This balance is critical: too much humility might risk complacency, while unchecked ambition could lead to reckless decisions. The key is to harness the strengths of both traits—let humility keep us focused on learning and improvement, and let hunger motivate us to pursue new heights.

As leaders, we must cultivate both humility and hunger in our approach. By staying humble, we keep ourselves open to learning from others and from our experiences, acknowledging there's always room for growth. By staying hungry, we ensure our leadership remains vibrant, pushing the boundaries of what we believe we can achieve. Coupled together, these qualities ensure we are always moving forward grounded in our values and driven by our visions. They prevent us from becoming too comfortable with past successes and motivate us to build on them, aspiring to bring out the best in ourselves and those we lead.

The Future Is Yours to Shape

The future may often seem like a distant, abstract concept, yet it is undeniably being molded by the decisions and actions we take today. This realization empowers us as leaders to actively participate in shaping what comes next, not only for ourselves but for our organizations and the communities we serve.

Consider what you want to be remembered for. Is it your integrity, your innovative spirit, or perhaps your commitment to nurturing others? Identifying what you want your legacy to be is the first step in living it out each day. Leadership is about more than handling the present; it's about envisioning and moving toward a future which aligns with your deepest values and aspirations. Every choice and action should reflect the kind of leader you aim to be, stitching a consistent thread through the narrative of your career.

Creating the future is about making intentional, purposeful decisions. It's about seeing beyond the immediate and considering the long-term impact of your actions. This strategic foresight involves understanding the implications of today's decisions and how they will echo into tomorrow. It means sometimes taking the harder right over the easier wrong, and planting seeds now for a harvest which many, including yourself, will reap years down the line.

Reflecting on the proverb, "The best time to plant a tree was 30 years ago. The second-best time is today," unknown, we are reminded of the urgency and importance of action. There's a natural tendency to think of the future as something which will come later, but the reality is the future is a series of 'nows'. Waiting for a perfect moment or delaying decisions for a more convenient time can mean missing out on valuable growth opportunities. Today is the best time to start laying the foundations of what you want to achieve.

As leaders, our task is to pioneer, to blaze trails, and pave pathways for others to follow. This doesn't just involve managing teams and tasks but also innovating, envisioning new possibilities, and taking bold steps forward. By adopting a pioneering mindset, you encourage a culture of progress and forward-thinking within your team or organization.

Ultimately, shaping the future is an active process which demands our engagement and dedication. It requires us to be visionary yet actionable, to dream big but also to ground those dreams in the realities of what we do today. As leaders, we have the unique opportunity to shape not just our destinies but also those of our teams

and organizations. Let's embrace this privilege with the urgency and commitment it deserves, knowing every moment is a chance to build a lasting legacy. And so, the journey continues as our conversation takes a pause (because, let's be honest, it's never really over), I hope you feel a renewed sense of purpose and excitement for the leadership journey ahead. It's a path filled with endless possibilities, challenges to overcome, and joyous victories to be had.

Remember, leadership is not a role or a title; it's an action, a behavior, and most importantly, a choice. It's the choice to make a positive impact, to inspire and empower those around you, and to leave a legacy that lasts long after you've moved on. Be so clear in your motives and intentions there remains no room left for suspicions or questions.

"The moment there is suspicion about a persons motives, everything he does becomes tainted."

- Mahatma Gandhi

So, here's to the road ahead, to the lessons we'll learn, and to the stories we'll tell. Keep leading with courage, compassion, and curiosity. Keep making those ripples and watch as they turn into waves. The journey of leadership is a beautiful one, and I can't wait to see where it takes you next.

Until our next chat, keep exploring, keep dreaming, and keep leading with heart. The best is yet to come, and I have no doubt that you'll make it amazing.

Onwards and upwards, my fellow traveler. The path of leadership awaits, and it's yours to walk with pride, purpose, and passion. Let's make it a journey to remember!

Chapter 9

Embracing The Winds Of Change: A Leader's Voyage

Isn't it fascinating how the winds of change can shift so swiftly? One moment you're sailing smoothly, and the next, you're adjusting your sails to catch the wind just right. Catching the wind just right was emphasized to me as an instructor when I attended the High-Altitude Aviation Training Site (HAATS) in Eagle, CO. Flying in the Rocky Mountains in a helicopter severely power limited by altitude gave me an appreciation for how birds use thermal updrafts to soar higher using minimal effort. Yes, they could flap harder to gain altitude but, you see minimal effort when you watch closely yet they climb higher and higher simply by using the wind. That's the beauty of leadership– it's as much about navigating change as it is about driving it. Let's keep riding these winds together, shall we?

Change: The Only Constant

Change is an undeniable force in both life and leadership. Here's the thing about change: it's the only constant. Whether it's new technology, shifting market dynamics, or a team member moving on, change keeps things interesting. Embrace it as an opportunity to innovate, to grow, and to strengthen your team, to become a more effective leader. Remember, a smooth sea never made a skilled sailor. It's the challenges that shape us, that teach us the most valuable lessons.

The natural instinct might be to resist change because it pulls us out of our comfort zones. However, embracing change is crucial. It presents a unique opportunity to innovate and grow, to test our strategies under new conditions, and to enhance our capabilities as leaders. When change occurs, it brings with it a chance to strengthen the team, fostering adaptability and resilience.

Change, often cited as the only true constant, is a principle vividly illustrated in the natural dynamics of a wolf pack. In the wilderness, the role of the Alpha is not static but subject to the inevitable shifts and turns of life. This leadership role, pivotal for the pack's survival and success, may pass from one member to another, dictated by various factors including age, strength, and strategic thinking. This transition is not merely a shift in power but a necessary adaptation which ensures the pack remains vigorous and capable of facing new challenges.

In the wolf pack, each member assumes roles which may change over time due to health, age, or external pressures. Such shifts are natural and vital for the pack's resilience. The Alpha, leading from behind, ensures no wolf is left behind, mirroring a deep understanding of each member's capabilities and the collective needs of the pack. When it's time for a new leader to emerge, the process reflects the pack's response to internal and external changes, ensuring their survival and continuity.

Similarly, in business and personal development, embracing the inevitability of change is crucial. Leaders must adapt, evolve, and sometimes step aside for new leadership to inject fresh ideas and approaches. This cyclical nature of change and leadership ensures a team or organization remains flexible and resilient, capable of navigating the complexities of an ever-changing environment. Just as in nature, the best leaders observe, adapt, and prepare not only themselves but their teams to thrive in a world where change is the only constant.

Understanding change is not just a hurdle but a gateway which can transform how we lead. It allows us to view each shift as a chance to improve—whether through integrating new technology to streamline operations, adjusting our approach to better fit changing market conditions, or finding fresh ways to motivate and engage a transitioning team.

Adopting an agile mindset is key when dealing with constant change. Agility in leadership means being prepared to pivot strategies, reassess goals, and innovate processes. It's about maintaining flexibility and being ready to seize the opportunities which change often conceals within its challenges.

Change tests our resilience. It challenges us to apply what we know in new ways and to learn rapidly what we don't yet understand. As the saying goes, "A smooth sea never made a skilled sailor." Similarly, it is the tempests of change which hone our skills and deepen our leadership qualities. Each challenge we navigate not only adds to our experience but also teaches us invaluable lessons about perseverance, decision-making, and crisis management.

Effective leaders anticipate change. They stay informed about trends and potential disruptions in their industries. This proactive approach allows them to guide their teams through transitions with confidence and foresight. By preparing for change, leaders can mitigate its impacts and harness its momentum to propel their team and organization forward.

Ultimately, our response to change defines our path in leadership. By embracing change with an open mind and a strategic approach, we can transform potential disruptions into powerful catalysts for growth and innovation. Remember, it is through navigating the ever-changing seas that we emerge not just as capable leaders but as architects of the future, continuously shaping and adapting the world around us.

Cultivating a Culture of Innovation

Innovation is much more than just brainstorming sessions or the relentless pursuit of 'the next big thing.' It's about creating fertile ground where new ideas can sprout, flourish, and transform into meaningful changes. This cultivating environment welcomes curiosity, supports creative risk-taking, and understands failure is often a stepping stone to success.

At the heart of a truly innovative culture is the encouragement to ask, 'What if?' and 'Why not?' These questions open the door to possibilities, pushing teams to look beyond conventional solutions and consider new, sometimes uncharted paths.

It's about encouraging your team to dream big, think outside the conventional boundaries, and not just accept the status quo but challenge it.

> *"Push yourself, because no one else is going to do it for you."*
>
> **- Unknown**

Innovative leaders promote an atmosphere where every team member feels safe and supported to voice their ideas, no matter how unconventional or nascent they may seem. This includes providing the tools and the time necessary to explore these ideas without the immediate pressure of return on investment (ROI) or other constraints that might stifle creative thinking.

A key aspect of fostering innovation is the understanding that not every attempt will result in success. Creating a space where it's okay to fail removes the fear of making mistakes. Instead, it encourages team members to experiment and learn from each outcome. This iterative process is crucial because it helps refine ideas and strategies through real-world testing, leading to more robust and effective innovations.

A shining example of leadership in fostering innovation is Ellen Ochoa, a veteran astronaut and the first Hispanic woman to go to space. During her tenure as the director of the Johnson Space Center, Ochoa emphasized the importance of innovation and teamwork in space exploration. She championed a diverse environment where collaborative efforts and creative solutions were essential to solving complex problems in space missions. Under her leadership, teams were encouraged to think differently, work closely across disciplines, and push the boundaries of what is technologically possible.

Leaders like Ellen Ochoa demonstrate today's

'wild ideas' can indeed become tomorrow's breakthroughs. By valuing diverse perspectives and fostering an environment where questioning and risk-taking are part of the daily process, leaders can unlock the potential of their teams and spearhead industry-leading innovations.

Ultimately, cultivating a culture of innovation is about much more than just generating new products or services; it's about instilling a mindset of continuous improvement and open-minded exploration across the organization. This approach not only leads to breakthroughs but also creates a dynamic workplace where employees are engaged, motivated, and committed to pushing the envelope, knowing they are part of a larger mission of transformation and growth.

Leadership Is a Team Sport

Leadership is fundamentally about unity; it's about bringing people together, rallying the crew, and navigating through challenges collectively. Just as no ship can sail without its crew, no leader can succeed without a dedicated team. The synergy between a leader and their team is what propels an organization forward, turning individual efforts into a powerful, unified force.

One of the greatest strengths of any team is the diversity of its members—not just in terms of demographics but also in thought, experience, and perspective. A wise leader recognizes and celebrates this diversity, understanding that a variety of viewpoints can enhance problem-solving capabilities and drive innovation. When you embrace and leverage the unique backgrounds and insights of your team members, you set the stage for creative solutions and a richer, more comprehensive approach to any challenge.

Trust is the cornerstone of effective leadership and teamwork. To establish trust…first, it is important to become consistent in your behavior, and your day-to-day actions. It's about more than just

believing in each other's abilities; it's about relying on each other's intentions and character. As a leader, your team looks to your actions as a benchmark for their own. By demonstrating reliability and integrity in your everyday behavior, you establish a standard and create an environment where trust can flourish.

Furthermore, trust is reinforced when leaders are self-aware and committed to personal growth. Leaders who are self-aware and continuously seek opportunities to improve gain the trust of their followers. Doing these things sets a powerful example for their teams but also signals their commitment to the collective success of the group. This ongoing development fosters respect and trust, as team members see a leader who is not only directing the team but also evolving with it.

It's crucial to remember trust isn't built overnight. It accumulates through sustained effort, consistent actions, and open communication. As you navigate through various challenges and successes together, trust deepens, strengthening the team's dynamics and enhancing its effectiveness.

The strongest teams are those built on a foundation of mutual support, respect, and understanding. As a leader, it's important to foster an environment where every team member feels valued and supported. This includes providing opportunities for growth, recognizing achievements, and encouraging open dialogue. When team members feel supported, they are more likely to contribute fully and collaborate more effectively.

Ultimately, leadership as a team sport is about setting a course together and facing the storms side by side. It's about deploying the collective power of the team to achieve common goals and overcome obstacles. By valuing diversity, building trust, and fostering an environment of support and respect, you ensure your leadership is not just a solo endeavor but a collaborative journey which brings out the best in everyone involved.

> *"The climb to the top may be rugged and littered with obstacles, reaching the top with your team and enjoying the view is well worth the effort."*
>
> - JDS

Finding Joy in the Journey

Amidst the hustle and bustle, don't forget to find joy in the journey. This role, often seen as a serious endeavor marked by objectives and outcomes, is also replete with opportunities for joy, laughter, and memorable experiences.

Leadership isn't just about milestones and achievements; it's about the laughter shared, the challenges overcome, and the memories made along the way (do you notice any reoccurring themes here?) It's important to remember these elements are not just byproducts of pursuing goals but are integral to the essence of leadership itself. The laughter shared in a team meeting, the sense of accomplishment after overcoming a tough challenge, or the quiet moments of camaraderie during a coffee break—these are as valuable as any formal recognition or achievement.

One key to finding joy in the journey is to recognize and celebrate small victories. These moments, whether they involve reaching a minor target or successfully implementing a small part of a larger project, are worth acknowledging and celebrating. They serve as reminders of progress and fuel motivation, but more importantly, they offer a chance to reflect on the growth that occurs along the way.

Taking time for reflection is another vital aspect of enjoying the leadership journey. Reflecting on where you started and the steps you have taken not only provides perspective but also deepens your appreciation for the process. Additionally, the camaraderie which develops from working closely with others toward common goals can be one of the most fulfilling aspects of leadership. This sense of belonging and mutual support is a profound source of joy.

Moreover, there's a unique satisfaction which comes from knowing you are part of something bigger than yourself...being part of an animal pack which successfully obtained a kill together. Leadership often involves guiding efforts which contribute to larger organizational visions or even societal change. The pride and fulfillment derived from this knowledge can make the day-to-day challenges of leadership more rewarding and enjoyable.

While leadership is undoubtedly filled with challenges and demands, it also offers numerous opportunities to find joy and fulfillment. By taking time to appreciate the small victories, savor the moments of laughter and connection, and reflect on the progress made, leaders can enrich their experience significantly. Remember, reoccurring themes of joy, camaraderie, and reflection are not coincidental—they are central to a fulfilling leadership journey. Embrace these elements and let them guide you to not only succeed but to enjoy each step of the path you're on.

"Talent wins games, but teamwork and intelligence win championships."

- Michael Jordan

The Overlap of Charisma and Leadership

Charisma and leadership, while distinct concepts, often intertwine to create a compelling force which can significantly elevate a leader's impact. Charisma —the magnetic appeal or charm which inspires devotion in others — can be a powerful component of effective leadership when aligned with strong leadership skills and ethical standards. Charisma can amplify a leader's ability to influence, motivate, and inspire their teams. It acts as a catalyst which not only attracts people but also engages and connects with them on a deeper level. This magnetic quality makes charismatic leaders highly effective in persuading their teams toward a vision or goal. However, charisma alone isn't enough for effective leadership; it must be coupled with integrity, strategic thinking, and genuine concern for others.

The most impactful leaders blend charisma with essential leadership qualities such as transparency, accountability, and empathy. When charisma is underpinned by a strong ethical framework and a commitment to organizational values, it contributes to a positive and motivating atmosphere. This combination helps foster trust and loyalty among team members, as they are drawn not only to the leader's allure but also to their vision and decisionmaking.

Different leaders exhibit charisma in various ways. Some may be charismatic through their passionate communication; others might exude a calm assurance which instills confidence without much fanfare. The key is understanding how to harness one's natural charisma to complement one's leadership style. This self-awareness allows leaders to authentically connect with their teams, adapting their approach to meet both the moment's needs and their personnel's.

An exemplary figure who demonstrates the effective meshing of charisma and leadership is Barack Obama. His charismatic ability to communicate, paired with his inclusive leadership style, allowed him to inspire a nation and drive significant change. Obama's charisma made his messages more compelling, but it was his substantive policies and steady leadership which won him trust and credibility.

While charisma can significantly enhance a leader's influence, its real value is realized when it's integrated with solid leadership qualities. The overlap of charisma and leadership creates a synergistic effect leading to high team engagement, strong motivation, and substantial organizational achievements. Leaders who manage to blend these traits effectively are not just admired— they are followed, for they offer a clear, inspiring vision and the reliable means to achieve it.

Following an interview as the Secretary of State, General Powell stated some wisdom he received as a young Lieutenant from one of his Sergeants at the

Infantry School: He said, "Lieutenant, you know you are a good leader when people follow you if only out of curiosity."

Ethical vs. Non-Ethical Use of Charisma in Leadership

Charisma, when harnessed correctly, can be a profound force for positive change and inspiration within an organization. However, the power of charisma also carries a significant responsibility, as its impact can sway large groups and shape organizational cultures for better or for worse.

Ethically using charisma involves leveraging this personal appeal to foster an inclusive, positive, and productive environment. Leaders who use their charisma ethically are marked by their commitment to transparency, integrity, and the greater good. They inspire and motivate their teams not just to meet organizational goals but to do so in a way that is fair, respectful, and sustainable.

Such leaders use their charm to unify teams, create bonds, and promote values that benefit all stakeholders. They listen actively, encourage open communication, and make decisions that reflect both their values and those of their organization. A prime example of ethical charisma in action is Nelson Mandela, whose magnetic personality and steadfast dedication to justice and equality inspired not just a nation but the entire world to embrace change and reconciliation.

Conversely, charisma can be used non-ethically when leaders employ their charm and influence to manipulate, coerce, or deceive others for personal gain or to advance their own agenda at the expense of others. Such leaders may prioritize their own visibility and success over the well-being of their teams and organizations. They might mask ulterior motives with their compelling presence, misleading followers towards goals that compromise ethical standards.

Non-ethical charismatic leadership can lead to a toxic work environment, where the focus shifts from collective achievement to personal power dynamics. Adolf Hitler is a historical example of how charismatic leadership, when coupled with destructive intentions and unethical practices, can lead to catastrophic outcomes.

To ensure the ethical use of charisma, leaders must balance their natural influence with a strong sense of accountability. This involves regular selfreflection and feedback mechanisms that keep their actions aligned with ethical practices and organizational values. Effective leaders set up checks and balances within their teams to ensure that their charismatic influence does not overpower the voices of others or lead to unchallenged decision-making.

Ultimately, the ethical use of charisma in leadership is about wielding influence with conscience and responsibility. It's about using personal appeal to positively impact and uplift, rather than manipulate or control. Leaders must strive to use their charisma to build trust genuinely, advocate for fair practices, and guide their teams with honesty and integrity. By doing so, they not only achieve success but also contribute to creating a more just and equitable workplace and society.

A New Chapter Awaits

As we wrap up this leg of our conversation, remember every day is a new chapter in your leadership journey. It's a chance to make a difference, to inspire change, and to leave a mark on the hearts and minds of those you lead.

Stay curious, stay humble, and stay driven. The world is full of opportunities for those willing to reach for them. Keep your eyes on the horizon, but don't forget to enjoy the view along the way. The path of leadership is rich with possibilities, challenges, and rewards.

Thank you for sharing this journey with me. Here's to the adventures that lie ahead, to the challenges we'll face, and to the stories we'll tell. Your leadership journey is uniquely yours, but remember, you're never alone on this path.

Until next time, keep steering your ship with courage, compassion, and conviction. The future is bright, and I can't wait to see where your leadership will take you.

Onwards to new horizons, my friend. The adventure continues, and the best is truly yet to come. Let's make it extraordinary, together.

Chapter 10

Leaning Into The Lessons: The Uncharted Territories Of Leadership

As we continue to navigate through the uncharted territories of leadership, it's the unexpected lessons which often provide the most profound insights. Leadership, after all, is a journey of constant learning, adapting, and growing. So, let's dive deeper into these lessons, shall we? The adventure is far from over.

The Art of Active Listening: Listen to Understand, Not To Simply Respond

There is one tool each leader should have in their toolkit of leadership skills which enhances effectiveness, active listening. It goes beyond the mechanics of hearing words; it's about engaging fully and understanding the deeper meanings behind what is being communicated. This skill is not just beneficial—it's foundational for building strong relationships and fostering a collaborative team environment.

Active listening involves a conscious effort to hear not only the words another person says but, more importantly, the complete message being communicated. This includes paying attention to body language, tone of voice, and emotional undertones, which often convey more than words alone. By truly listening, leaders can grasp the nuances of team dynamics, individual concerns, and underlying issues which may not be explicitly stated.

One of the most significant benefits of active listening is the trust it builds between leaders and their teams. When team members feel heard and understood, they are more likely to open up and share their true thoughts and feelings. This trust is crucial for creating an open and transparent workplace where people feel safe to express themselves without fear of judgment or reprisal.

Moreover, active listening often reveals insights which might otherwise remain hidden. Team members can offer unexpected solutions, novel ideas, or critical observations which could lead to breakthroughs in projects or improvements in processes. These "diamonds in the rough" can be invaluable, making the difference between a good team and a great one.

When leaders practice active listening, they send a powerful message to their team: "You are valued." This creates a strong sense of belonging and commitment among team members. People who feel their contributions are acknowledged and their opinions respected are more engaged and motivated. They're also more likely to exhibit loyalty to the team and go above and beyond in their roles.

To practice active listening, start by focusing completely on the speaker. Avoid distractions, maintain eye contact, and nod or give small verbal affirmations to show you're engaged. Importantly, listen with the intent to understand, not just to reply. This means refraining from planning what to say next while the other person is speaking.

Instead, absorb the full message being conveyed.

After listening, reflect back on what you've heard and ask clarifying questions to deepen your understanding. This reflection not only confirms you've understood but also enriches your grasp of the content and context of the conversation.

Active listening is more than a skill—it's an art which requires practice, patience, and genuine interest in the perspectives of others. By mastering this art, leaders can transform their interactions and relationships, leading to a more collaborative, innovative, and supportive work environment. The next time you engage in a conversation, remember: the most effective response is often found not in the words you speak but in the silence which shows you're truly listening.

"I remind myself every morning: Nothing I say this day will teach me anything. So, if I'm going to learn, I must do it by listening."

- Larry King, CNN

Embracing the Role of Chief Encouragement Officer

As a leader, one of your most impactful roles is that of the Chief Encouragement Officer. We could just call it what it is, Head Cheerleader. This role isn't about empty pep talks, it's deeply rooted in the genuine belief in your team's potential, especially at those times when they're filled with self-doubt.

It's all about highlighting their hard work, throwing a party (even if it's just metaphorical) for their wins, and being the steadfast coach who gets them through the rough patches. Being the Chief Encouragement Officer isn't just about issuing pats on the back; your encouragement is the force which lifts them, pushing your team to stretch their boundaries and climb to higher heights. And don't forget, the power of dropping a heartfelt "I believe in you" at the right moment can work miracles.

Picture the iconic leaders who've made a difference in the world or even in your life. More often than not, their legacy is built on how they've uplifted others, how they've turned doubt into confidence, and challenges into stepping stones for their team. It's this relentless support and belief in their people's abilities that has propelled teams to achieve greatness.

So, as you navigate your leadership journey, remember, your role as the Chief Encouragement Officer is pivotal. It's not just about directing or managing—it's about inspiring, believing, and empowering. Whether it's through celebrating small victories or offering a shoulder to lean on during setbacks, your encouragement makes all the difference. It's what turns a group of individuals into an unstoppable team. Never underestimate the power of a simple "I believe in you."

> *"No matter the time of day or night, no matter your location on this planet, no matter your status or title, everyone can use encouragement."*
>
> *- JDS*

Navigating Through Failures with Grace

Failures are as much a part of the leadership journey as successes. While setbacks can oftentimes be challenging and disheartening, the true measure of a leader's strength is often seen in how they navigate and manage these turbulent times. It's not just about bouncing back; it's about moving forward with increased determination, wisdom, and resilience.

One of the first steps in dealing with failure gracefully is maintaining your composure. This doesn't mean suppressing emotions or pretending everything is fine— it means acknowledging the situation without letting it overwhelm you or your team. By staying calm and composed, you provide a sense of stability for your team, reassuring them that setbacks are manageable and surmountable.

Every failure carries a lesson, and part of navigating setbacks with grace involves extracting these lessons and sharing them with your team. This process begins with a thorough analysis of what went wrong and why. Was it a flaw in planning? Was there a mismatch in team roles? Did external factors play a role? Understanding these elements not only helps in correcting course but also prevents future mistakes.

Once the lessons are learned, the next step is to pivot with grace.

This means making the necessary adjustments to strategies and plans without drama or unnecessary fanfare. It involves a straightforward, thoughtful approach that shows your team how to adapt and evolve in response to challenges. This can be an incredibly powerful model for your team, showing them that it's possible to make course corrections without losing momentum or focus.

Encourage your team to embrace a mindset of 'failing forward.' This concept is about using each failure as a stepping stone towards greater success.

It's about iterative learning—constantly improving and refining processes based on past outcomes. When leaders openly embrace this approach, it creates a culture where team members are not afraid to take calculated risks or try new things, knowing that their efforts are valued more than the immediate results.

In any journey, particularly one as rigidly structured as a military career, being resilient demonstrates the simple yet profound act of showing up. This foundational principle was a cornerstone of my tenure at the Army Human Resources Command, where I had the privilege of traveling globally as part of the command team, engaging directly with our nation's warriors. Our discussions often revolved around key operational themes such as personnel numbers, professional growth, stewardship of the profession, and promotions. Yet, based on insightful feedback from senior leaders, I made it a point to insert a crucial topic: the imperative to show up.

Your reaction to failures not only teaches your team how to deal with setbacks but also inspires them to persevere. Show them that resilience is about more than enduring; it's about emerging stronger and more capable on the other side of adversity. Your strength and grace in handling these situations motivate your team to push through their limitations and emerge more cohesive and empowered.

Navigating through failures with grace is a crucial skill for any leader. It transforms potential negatives into powerful opportunities for growth and team building. By maintaining composure, learning from each setback, pivoting with purpose, and encouraging a culture of failing forward, you set a standard of resilience and continuous improvement. This approach not only helps in overcoming current challenges but also prepares your team for future success, reinforcing the idea that true leadership is defined not by an unbroken string of successes, but by the ability to navigate the inevitable lows with wisdom and grace.

Robert F. Smith is an excellent example of an African American male who has navigated through failures with grace and achieved remarkable success.

Robert F. Smith is the founder, chairman, and CEO of Vista Equity Partners, a private equity firm which focuses primarily on investing in technology companies. Smith's journey is a testament to resilience and strategic thinking in the face of challenges.

Born in Denver, Colorado, Smith trained as an engineer at Cornell University and later earned his MBA from Columbia Business School. His early career included working at Kraft General Foods as a chemical engineer, where he earned two United States and two European patents. After discovering his interest in business and finance, Smith faced the monumental challenge of breaking into investment banking, a field not known for its diversity at the time.

Smith started in technology investment banking at Goldman Sachs, where he advised on mergers and acquisitions and financing for tech companies. Despite the dog-eat-dog nature of Wall Street and the additional hurdles he faced as an African

American in the industry, Smith excelled by focusing on the tech sector during the early days of the internet.

In 2000, he founded Vista Equity Partners, which would become one of the most successful private equity firms specializing in technology investments. The road to building Vista was not smooth; the early 2000s were a turbulent time for technology investments, with the dot-com bubble bursting shortly after Vista was founded. However, Smith's strategic focus on enterprise software, an area less susceptible to market whims than consumer tech, allowed Vista to not only survive but thrive.

Robert F. Smith's story illustrates how resilience, strategic foresight, and ethical leadership can drive success and make a significant impact in technology, finance, and philanthropy. His journey is particularly inspiring for showing how grace and determination can overcome challenges and lead to meaningful achievements, both personally and professionally.

The Military Foundation: Commitment to Presence

In the military, showing up goes beyond mere physical presence. It's a commitment to be fully engaged and ready, regardless of your role, rank, or the specific cohort you belong to—be it Enlisted, Warrant Officer, Commissioned Officer, or Department of the Army

Civilian. It was starting to be a reoccurring issue as we traveled…a particular group wasn't showing up, and they were not visible at professional development, PT, etc.; This was truly impactful however, it was a negative impact which needed to be addressed immediately as perceptions were demonstrating a negative reality which was not systemic. It just appeared in isolated communities, but word of mouth presented a different tale.

I included in my briefings to the audiences that signing on the dotted line is more than a formality; it's a pledge to be present, accountable, and prepared to contribute to the mission at hand. This act of showing up sets the stage for all aspects of military operation and ethos, fostering a culture of reliability and readiness which is essential in high-

stakes environments. Showing up meant understanding eyes are watching with expectations attached. These eyes sought sage advice, mentorship, and active participation in all unit functions. We needed to change the perception and for those of us on the command team, it began with us.

> *"Not everything that is faced can be changed, but nothing can be changed until it is faced."*
>
> **- James Baldwin**

Parallel to the Business World: The Value of Reliability

In the world of business, just as in the military, the principle of showing up—both in presence and participation—holds unprecedented value. This concept of reliability is foundational to the success of any organization, influencing everything from team dynamics to overall company performance.

As the corporate world increasingly adopts virtual and hybrid work models, the meaning of 'showing up' was forced to evolve. It's no longer just about being physically present in an office setting; it's about being fully engaged and contributing actively, whether from a distance or in person. In these shifting work environments, the re liability of each team member becomes even more crucial. Being dependable, meeting deadlines, staying communicative, and maintaining productivity from any location are all facets of how employees today can demonstrate their commitment and reliability.

Employees who consistently demonstrate reliability are invaluable to their organizations. They are often viewed as the backbone of team projects, driving initiatives forward with their staunch dedication. Their dependable nature ensures work progresses smoothly, obstacles are managed efficiently, and goals are met on time. This consistency not only enhances the group's overall effectiveness but also boosts team morale, creating an environment where trust and mutual respect are paramount.

Reliability also intersects deeply with company values. Employees who show up reliably embody these principles through their actions, reinforcing the company's culture and ethos in everything they do. This embodiment of core values is crucial, as it influences not just their work but also sets a standard for others. Furthermore, reliable employees often naturally step into leadership roles, regardless of their official title. Their dependability and commitment inspire confidence, making them leaders among their peers and trusted voices within their organizations.

In today's diverse and dynamic business environments, the value of reliability cannot be overstated. It is a key trait which transcends physical presence, embracing a proactive, engaged, and consistent approach to work. For companies navigating the complexities of modern business practices, fostering a culture which prizes reliability is essential. It ensures not only the smooth operation of day-to-day activities but also builds a resilient foundation for the organization's future.

By nurturing and recognizing reliability in employees, businesses can maintain high standards of performance and morale, regardless of where or how work is being done. It's clear that reliability remains one of the most valued attributes in any professional setting, acting as a significant determinant of individual and collective success.

From Military to Management: Leadership Lessons

Leaders in the business world can draw direct inspiration from military practices by encouraging a culture where showing up is recognized and valued. This involves not only acknowledging the physical or virtual presence but also cultivating an environment where employees are mentally and emotionally engaged. Leaders should emphasize the importance of each team member's contribution, reinforcing everyone's role is crucial to the collective success of the organization.

Ultimately, the concept of showing up, ingrained deeply within military training and operations, transcends contexts and is applicable to any field, particularly in leadership and management. It is about making a conscious decision to be present, to be fully engaged, and to commit oneself to the task and team. Whether on the field or in the office, the ability to show up and deliver consistently forms the backbone of both individual success and organizational achievement.

By nurturing and recognizing reliability in employees, businesses can maintain high standards of performance and morale, regardless of where or how work is being done. It's clear that reliability remains one of the most valued attributes in any professional setting, acting as a significant determinant of individual and collective success. By maintaining this focus on the fundamental act of showing up, we continue to bridge the gap between military discipline and business efficiency, offering a robust framework for leadership and commitment which resonates across both spheres.

The Path Forward: Charting Your Course with Confidence

As we venture forward on this leadership journey, let's chart our course with confidence, guided by the lessons we've learned and the experiences we've shared. The path may not always be clear, and the se as may not always be calm, but with a steadfast spirit and an open heart, there's no storm we can't weather together. A steadfast spirit in leadership means maintaining your focus and drive, even when the path becomes unclear. It's about demonstrating to your team that with determination and adaptability, obstacles can be transformed into stepping stones toward greater achievements. This spirit inspires confidence in your team, emboldening them with the courage to pursue ambitious goals and innovate without fear.

Business Applications: Navigating Uncertainty

In the business landscape, charting a course with confidence means making strategic decisions based on both accumulated wisdom and forward-looking insights. In the ever-changing terrain of the business world, navigating uncertainty with confidence is not just an advantage; it's a necessity. It involves not just reacting to market changes but proactively planning for future possibilities. By applying our learned experiences—much like a captain uses charts and instruments—we can develop the intelligence to anticipate trends, adapt strategies, and steer our organizations toward sustained success.

Effective leadership in business resembles the skilled captain of a ship, who must use both charts and instincts to navigate through uncharted waters. This analogy highlights the importance of integrating accumulated knowledge with forwardlooking insights to guide decision-making. Leaders must draw on their experiences and historical data to understand trends, but they also need to stay attuned to emerging technologies, market shifts, and global economic indicators that could impact their strategic direction.

Proactive planning for the future involves more than cautious risk management; it requires a visionary approach which embraces innovation and seeks opportunities in the face of ambiguity. By cultivating a mindset which views uncertainty not as a barrier but as an invitation to innovate, leaders can transform potential threats into growth opportunities. This proactive stance enables businesses to remain agile and adaptable, ready to pivot strategies as needed to capitalize on emerging trends.

Just as a captain uses sophisticated instruments to navigate, modern businesses must utilize advanced business intelligence tools and analytics to forecast trends and inform strategies. These tools allow leaders to analyze vast amounts of data to identify patterns which could signify upcoming changes in consumer behavior, supply chain disruptions, or competitive dynamics. Armed with this intelligence, businesses can adjust their strategies in real-time, ensuring they remain relevant and competitive.

This strategic approach to navigating uncertainty not only builds confidence but also strengthens organizational resilience. By preparing for multiple scenarios and cultivating flexibility within their strategic plans, businesses can withstand shocks and stressors which might otherwise destabilize them. Furthermore, leaders who demonstrate confidence and clarity in their decision-making inspire trust and loyalty among stakeholders, enhancing team cohesion and collective resilience. Mastering the art of navigating uncertainty in the business world requires a blend of experienced judgment and innovative foresight. Leaders must be adept at interpreting the signs of change and skilled in adjusting their sails accordingly. By applying learned experiences and embracing proactive planning, businesses can steer a steady course through the complexities of modern markets, achieving sustained success and resilience in an unpredictable world.

This approach not only demonstrates the importance of confidence in navigating the future but also highlights practical strategies for applying these principles in the business world, enhancing both personal leadership and organizational resilience.

Keep Your Compass Pointed Towards Your Values

In the ever-changing landscape of leadership, let your values be your compass. They will guide you through ethical dilemmas, tough decisions, and moments of uncertainty. When you're true to your values, you'll never lose your way, no matter how tumultuous the journey is.

Leadership involves navigating through a myriad of decisions which can have profound impacts on your team, organization, and broader community. In this ever-changing landscape, your values are not just personal principles; they are your ethical guideposts. They help you maneuver through ethical dilemmas and tough decision-making processes with integrity and consistency. When values such as honesty, fairness, and responsibility are deeply ingrained in your leadership approach, they ensure that every choice you make aligns with these fundamental beliefs.

Moments of uncertainty often test a leader's character and decision-making clarity. In such times, your values become particularly crucial. They provide a clear pathway when the road ahead is obscured by complexity or ambiguity. By keeping your compass pointed towards your values, you ensure that no matter how tumultuous the journey, your actions remain true to what you stand for, fostering trust and respect among your peers and subordinates.

Being consistent in living out your values in all aspects of leadership builds an environment of trust and predictability. This consistency reassures your team that, regardless of external pressures or challenges, you will lead in a manner which is not only effective but also ethically sound. This trust is crucial for fostering a positive organizational culture where all members feel secure and valued, knowing that their leaders will always act in accordance with declared values.

Moreover, when leaders demonstrate a strong commitment to their values, they inspire their teams to embody these ideals as well. This inspiration can motivate employees to strive for excellence, engage more deeply with their work, and contribute to a positive and ethical working environment. Leaders who exemplify their values in action can ignite a powerful sense of purpose and dedication among their team members.

Keeping your compass directed towards your values is not just about personal integrity; it's about setting a standard for ethical leadership which resonates throughout your entire organization. Your values are your most reliable navigational tools—they help you lead with confidence, steer through adversity, and leave a legacy of principled leadership. By remaining true to your values, you ensure that no matter the challenges, your leadership path will lead toward positive outcomes and enduring respect.

Cultivate a Spirit of Adventure

Approach leadership with a spirit of adventure. Embrace the unknown with excitement, see challenges as opportunities for growth, and remain curious about the world around you. This adventurous spirit will not only make the journey more enjoyable but also inspire those you lead to explore their own potential.

Never Stop Exploring, Learning, and Growing

The journey of leadership is an endless expedition of exploration, learning, and growth. There will always be new horizons to discover, new challenges to face, and new lessons to learn. Embrace this continuous journey with enthusiasm and an eagerness to evolve.

> *"Do the best you can until you know better. Then when you know better, do better."*
>
> **- Maya Angelou**

A Heartfelt Thank You

As we pause in our conversation, know that the journey doesn't end here. It continues in every decision you make, every challenge you face, and every life you touch.

Your leadership is a gift—not just to your team, but to the world.

Thank you for embracing this journey with openness, courage, and a willingness to make a difference. Here's to the roads we've traveled and the paths yet to be explored. May your leadership journey be filled with purpose, passion, and endless possibilities.

Until we meet again on this journey, keep leading with heart, embracing the adventures that await, and always moving forward with confidence. The world is a better place with you at the helm. We are about to change our lens, prepare yourself for the ride!

Chapter 11

Let's Take To The Sky

Charting New Horizons: The Aviator's Guide to Leadership

As we continue our leadership journey, pull up your chair, refresh your drink, and let's take to the skies viewing leadership through the lens of an aviator and couple it with some aviation jargon. Just as a pilot navigates through ever-changing conditions to reach their destination, so too does a leader guide their team through the uncertainties of the business world. Let's soar together, exploring the vast skies of leadership with an aviation twist.

As a pilot, when I am flying high above the clouds,

I have a perspective that's both broad and focused, navigating through storms, adjusting to shifting winds, and always keeping the destination in mind. On the flight deck, every decision counts, every adjustment is calculated, and yet, there's a calm, almost casual confidence which comes from knowing the airplane, crew, and my capabilities. It's this aviator mindset that, when applied to the business world, can truly transform the way we approach challenges and opportunities.

Drawing these parallels from the aviation world offers valuable insights into how adopting an aviator's mindset can significantly enhance business strategies and thought processes. It can simply "Change How You Think." It's about embracing preparation, awareness, adaptability, and clear communication as the cornerstones of successful leadership. Just as pilots navigate the skies with confidence and skill, so too can business leaders chart their course through the corporate landscape with the same level of expertise and calm assurance. This is a feeling you get when you have invested with your all, with your heart.

Flying is not solely about navigating by instruments and calculations; it's also about feeling the aircraft and its behavior in different conditions—intuitive knowledge which comes from experience and from a deep connection with flying.

Similarly, leading with the heart involves understanding and relating to people not just through policies and strategies but through shared feelings, experiences, and values.

In conclusion, just as flying satisfies a deeper, almost spiritual need beyond the technical aspects of aviation, leading with the heart taps into a more profound part of our humanity than cerebral management ever could. It's about engaging with the world and with others in a way that satisfies our deepest desires for connection and impact, illustrating that sometimes, what drives us forward isn't found in thought, but in feeling.

The Infinite Sky: A Leader's Playground

Let's take some time to imagine the sky as this vast, boundless expanse where the only limits are the ones we set for ourselves. In the world of leadership, this sky isn't just a backdrop; it's the ultimate playground. Think about it—the excitement of charting a path to unknown destinations, the buzz of discovering unexplored territories, and the exhilarating sense of steering your team into these new horizons.

Leadership, in many ways, mirrors the audacious spirit of aviation. Every day throws open the doors to fresh opportunities, new problems to solve, and novel ideas to pursue. It's about embracing the unknown with open arms and a spirit of curiosity. Just as a pilot traversing changing skies, a leader navigates the evolving landscapes of business and innovation.

This playground in the sky is where you get to test your limits, push your boundaries, and see how far you can really go. It's about finding new ways to inspire your team, dreaming up solutions that haven't been thought of yet, and having the courage to pursue them. The sky's vastness encourages us to think big, to aim high, and to remember that every challenge is just an adventure waiting to be conquered.

In this endless expanse, each day is a chance to fly a little higher, to explore a little further, and to grow a little stronger. Whether it's launching a daring new project, pivoting strategies in response to the prevailing winds of change, or nurturing a culture of innovation within your team, the sky—your playground—offers the perfect setting for leadership to take flight and explore the potential of what can be achieved.

In this vast playground of the sky, where every cloud, every gust of wind, and every ray of sunlight offers a new perspective, leaders find their true calling. It's a realm where the thrill of the journey is just as important as the destination, inviting leaders and their teams to spread their wings and soar toward the endless possibilities which await.

> *"If you can't stop thinking about it, don't stop working for it."*
>
> **--Unknown**

Crew Resource Management: The Value of Teamwork

Just as on the Flight deck where crew resource management is the cornerstone of a safe and successful flight, in the world of business, especially in handling customer relations, the power of teamwork can't be overstated or overlooked. It's all about bringing together diverse skills, experiences, and perspectives, much like assembling a top-notch flight crew to take flight lead on a military mission involving multiple aircraft flying into enemy airspace, they play a pivotal role. In this setup, fostering an environment of open dialogue, mutual respect, and shared problem-solving isn't just beneficial; it's essential.

Think of your team as a crew on a mission, where the collective effort is what keeps you flying high and on course. It's about more than just getting along—it's about each member knowing their role, understanding the bigger picture, and how they fit into it and can ultimately impact the outcome. This unity and coordination are what ensure not only the smooth running of day-to-day operations but also the seamless execution of larger strategic goals.

Drawing from the military's approach to crew resource management, the idea extends to creating multiple 'flight crews' within your organization. Each crew, or team, operates within its own domain but is intricately linked to the broader mission. The challenge—and the opportunity—lies in coordinating these teams in such a way that they not only achieve their individual objectives, but each crew helps to shape the battle space which also contributes to the overarching strategic goals. It's about harnessing the collective prowess of these teams, through targeted resource allocation and training, to achieve multifaceted objectives simultaneously.

In Customer Relations Management (CRM), this coordinated team effort married with technology translates into a seamless, holistic customer experience.

Each interaction, whether it's with sales, support, or service, is a touch point which reflects the efficiency and unity of the entire team. Just as a flight crew's coordinated efforts to ensure a safe and pleasant journey for passengers, a wellsynced customer relations team ensures a satisfying and loyal relationship with customers.

By leveraging the principles of crew resource management, businesses can foster a culture of collaboration and efficiency which echoes through every level of operation. This approach not only elevates the team's performance but also enhances customer satisfaction, driving towards the ultimate goal of achieving strategic objectives while maintaining a high level of service excellence.

Chapter 12

Preflight And Leaving The Gate, Let's Fly

Pre-Flight Checks: The Importance of Preparation

Before every takeoff, pilots perform flight planning and brief, pre-flight checks, taxi and departure brief, and a series of additional checks ensuring everything is in working order prior to taking the runway for departure. Similarly, in leadership, preparation is key. It's about knowing your team, understanding your objectives, and having a clear plan of action. Just like how every dial and gauge in the Flight deck provides crucial information, every piece of feedback, every data point, and every team interaction informs your leadership decisions. Ensure your leadership journey is well-prepared for takeoff by doing your due diligence and planning ahead.

When we consider the pilot's pre-flight checklist, we can consider its application to the business world. In business, this equates to thorough preparation before launching a project or strategy— understanding the market conditions, knowing your team's strengths and weaknesses, and having a clear plan of action. It's about minimizing risks through diligent preparation and foresight.

Ground Taxi: A Critical Phase of Operation

Navigating the runway before takeoff and after landing—known as ground taxiing in aviation—is a critical yet often overlooked phase of flight. It's a time when precision, awareness, and planning are paramount, ensuring the aircraft safely reaches the runway or the gate. This painstakingly meticulous journey on the ground mirrors an essential phase in business: the preparation and follow-through surrounding major initiatives or projects.

In the business world, ground taxiing represents the strategic planning and groundwork which precedes the launch of a project, as well as the debriefing and integration of lessons learned afterward. Just as a pilot must carefully navigate the tarmac, avoiding obstacles and following a predefined path to the runway, business leaders must conscientiously plan their approach to new ventures. This includes aligning resources, setting clear objectives, and preparing the team for the takeoff.

Takeoff: Set Thrust, Rotate, We Are Off

Takeoff and climb out in aviation—a phase filled with anticipation, acceleration, and the critical transition from ground to air—serves as a powerful metaphor for business initiatives and growth phases. This moment in a flight encapsulates the culmination of preparation, the execution of plans, and the exhilarating ascent toward cruising altitude, where the journey toward the destination really begins.

In the business context, takeoff represents the launch of a new project, product, or strategy. It's that thrilling phase where planning meets action, and ideas begin to take flight. Just like an aircraft needs the right speed, thrust, and trajectory to successfully take off, a business initiative requires the right mix of resources, momentum, and direction. The exhilaration felt as wheels leave the runway mirrors the collective energy and focus of a team as their hard work morphed from the mere idea to materialization in action.

The climb out, following takeoff, is equally significant. It's about gaining altitude, adjusting the initial trajectory as necessary, and navigating through any weather or turbulence encountered during the climb out. For businesses, this is mirroring the phase immediately following a launch—monitoring progress, making real-time adjustments based on feedback and early results, and overcoming initial challenges. It's a critical time when agility and responsiveness can make or break the trajectory of growth.

During this phase, the importance of clear communication and strong leadership cannot be overlooked or overstated. Just as a pilot must be in constant communication with air traffic control and the crew during takeoff and climb, business leaders must maintain open lines of communication with their teams and stakeholders. This ensures everyone remains aligned, focused, and ready to address any challenges head-on.

The parallels between aviation's takeoff and climb out and business launches and growth initiatives highlight the dynamics and resilience required to navigate these critical phases successfully. Both demand a deeper understanding of the conditions, the ability to adapt swiftly, and the courage to ascend boldly towards the objectives.

By drawing inspiration from the precision and determination inherent in a successful takeoff and climb, business leaders can approach their ventures with the same clarity and confidence, ready to soar towards their strategic goals with the entire team aligned and engaged for the journey ahead.

Flight Plan Adjustments: Being Flexible and Adaptable

Just as in aviation, where no flight plan is set in stone, leadership requires a similar degree of flexibility and adaptability in the business world.

Unforeseen challenges like Murphy's Law and Mother Nature can swiftly necessitate changes to even the most well-laid plans. Weather conditions change, and detours may be necessary. Leadership requires similar flexibility. Be prepared to adjust your strategies, pivot your approach, and explore new routes to achieve your goals.

In the world of aviation, pilots must continuously adjust their flight paths due to dynamic weather conditions or air traffic updates. These adjustments are crucial not just for the safety of the flight but also for its efficiency and effectiveness in reaching the intended destination. Similarly, in leadership, the ability to pivot strategies and adapt to changing circumstances is vital. Whether responding to market shifts, technological advancements, or internal team dynamics, effective leaders must be prepared to alter their course and explore new avenues for achieving their goals.

Just as a skilled pilot uses instruments to navigate through unforeseen changes, leaders rely on their knowledge, experience, and resources to guide their teams through challenges. By empowering your team to think creatively and propose new solutions, you cultivate an environment where new ideas can take flight. This not only enhances problem-solving capabilities but also ensures your organization remains competitive and responsive to opportunities.

The concept of strategic flexibility is akin to an aviator's adaptability. Aviators are adept at adjusting their course based on real-time information and conditions, understanding that while the final destination remains the same, the path to reaching it may vary significantly. In business, this translates to leaders possessing the agility to pivot strategies and remain flexible in their approach. This flexibility might mean adopting new technologies, overhauling old processes, or steering the company culture in a new direction to better align with contemporary challenges and opportunities.

Leaders who embrace flexibility and adaptability can navigate their organizations through uncertain waters and guide them to success, much like a pilot ensures their passengers reach their destination safely. This might involve taking uncharted routes or making difficult decisions which require departing from the original plan. However, the core objective remains the same: to lead the organization towards its goals, no matter the obstacles.

Leadership, much like piloting, demands a high level of adaptability and the ability to make realtime adjustments. Leaders must be as proficient in changing their strategies as pilots are in altering their flight paths. By embracing flexibility, encouraging innovation, and using their "instruments" wisely, leaders can ensure their teams remain resilient and goal-oriented, capable of reaching their destinations successfully, regardless of the turbulence encountered along the way.

> *"When obstacles arise, you change your direction to reach your goal; you do not change your decision to get there."*

> **- Zig Ziglar**

Navigating Through Turbulence: Staying Steady Amidst Challenges

Turbulence is an unavoidable part of flying, just as challenges are in leadership. The key is not to avoid turbulence but to navigate through it with skill and composure. Pilots and air traffic controllers must communicate succinctly and clearly to avoid misunderstandings. For business leaders, effective communication is equally vital, whether it's aligning the team on goals, negotiating with partners, or engaging with customers. Clear, concise, and open communication fosters a collaborative environment where ideas rise, the organization ascends to higher heights, and objectives are met with precision.

Just as pilots fly their aircraft, directing your organization is your primary duty as CEOs, Senior Executives, or Established Entrepreneurs. Keep a steady hand on the controls, make informed decisions, and maintain your course. Your ability to remain calm and collected during turbulent times will inspire confidence in your team and ensure a smoother journey for everyone onboard. Catastrophic mistakes are made when everyone is reacting to an emergency (looking inside), and no one maintains focus on the controls to fly the aircraft. As the leader, you must ensure someone is always on or monitoring the flight controls of your organization.

The View from the Flight Deck: Maintaining Perspective

Imagine the flight deck view, where the pilot navigates not just by the stretch of sky immediately ahead but also by the vast horizon which frames their journey. This dual perspective—eying the close-up details while keeping the broader picture in mind—is a powerful metaphor for leadership. It's about striking the fine balance between managing the nitty-gritty of daily tasks and steering towards the loftier goals on the horizon.

In the world of leadership, encouraging your team to adopt this flight deck view is key. It's not just about plowing through today's to-do list; it's about understanding how each task fits into the bigger picture. Inspire your crew with visions of what lies beyond the immediate horizon. Show them how their efforts today are paving the way for the bigger picture, aligning everyone's sights on the collective destination.

As you progress, the landscape shifts, and with every milestone reached, new opportunities unfold. This evolving view allows you, as the leader, to gradually step back from the minutiae of daily operations, granting you the bandwidth to focus more on strategic planning and scaling your business. It's akin to climbing higher in the atmosphere, where the view widens and you can see further into the distance, enabling you to chart a course that not only navigates the present but also shapes the future.

This broader perspective is invaluable. It enables leaders to anticipate changes, seize opportunities, and guide their teams through turbulence toward clear skies. It's about maintaining that delicate balance between the immediate and the infinite, ensuring while your hands are on the controls of day-to-day operations, your eyes are firmly fixed on the horizon, leading your team towards exciting new destinations.

By embracing this flight deck perspective, leaders can cultivate a forward-looking approach within their teams, ensuring that while the immediate tasks are handled with precision, there is always an awareness of and alignment with the long-term vision. This approach not only motivates and inspires but also sets the groundwork for sustained growth and success.

From the Flight deck, a pilot has a unique view, seeing both the immediate path ahead and the broader horizon. In leadership, maintaining perspective is crucial. It's about balancing day-today operations with long-term visions. Keep an eye on your immediate tasks but don't lose sight of your ultimate destination. Encourage your team to also look beyond the horizon, inspiring them with what lies ahead, and ensuring everyone is aligned with the mission.

This will allow you as a leader to cast your sights even further onto the horizon. With each evolution in your organization, opportunities arise which will allow you as a leader to remove yourself from the day-to-day operations to focus on strategic visions. This provides you as a leader with the ability to scale and grow your business.

Chapter 13

Cruising Altitude: The Stewardship Of Leadership

As we level off at cruising altitude, let's turn our conversation towards a critical aspect of the leadership journey—stewardship. Stewardship, in the context of leadership, is about caring for and nurturing the profession, ensuring it remains robust, respected, and relevant for future

generations. It's a commitment not just to lead but to protect, preserve, and enhance the leadership landscape.

In those stretches of smooth sailing, when projects are on track and operations are humming along nicely on autopilot, a golden opportunity emerges that's too valuable to miss—the chance to simply talk with your team. It's during these quieter moments, free from the immediate pressures of deadlines and decisions, that leaders can engage in more personal, meaningful conversations with their team members.

These discussions go beyond the usual status updates and task delegations. They're an opening to delve into topics like career aspirations, personal growth, feedback, and even the occasional off-topic interests that bring out the human side of the workplace. It's a chance to reinforce the bond with your team, showing them, they're valued not just for their work output but for who they are as individuals.

Think of it as the cruising altitude in a flight—a time when the fasten seatbelt sign is off, and passengers feel free to stretch their legs and chat with the cabin crew.

Similarly, when things are running smoothly in the business, it's an ideal time for leaders to walk the floor, have a coffee with a team member, or initiate team-building activities that foster a sense of community and belonging.

These conversations can also serve as an informal yet effective way to gauge team morale, gather insights on workflow improvements, or simply to offer a listening ear. They can illuminate hidden talents within your team, spark innovative ideas, or address small concerns before they grow into larger issues.

Moreover, taking the initiative to engage in these conversations demonstrates a leadership style that values openness, trust, and the well-being of its team members. It sets a tone that encourages everyone to contribute their best, knowing they are supported and heard. Embracing these periods of calm to connect with your team not only strengthens the fabric of your team's culture but also lays the groundwork for more resilient, motivated, and cohesive group dynamics. It's a reminder that, even when the business is cruising smoothly, the work of building and nurturing your team is never on autopilot.

Navigating the Responsibility

Leadership, like piloting, encompasses a significant responsibility that extends beyond oneself. A pilot's duty spans the safety of every soul on board, the integrity of the aircraft, and the environmental impact of every flight. Similarly, a leader's role involves a deep commitment to stewardship over their profession and their influence on the people and world around them.

At the core of effective leadership lies the principle of stewardship. Leaders, much like pilots, are entrusted with precious cargo—their team members, the organizational culture, and the broader impact of their decisions. This stewardship requires a commitment to uphold and promote ethical practices within every level of the organization.

It involves continuous learning and personal growth to ensure decisions are informed and reflective of best practices in leadership.

Leaders must actively cultivate a culture which prioritizes integrity, respect, and inclusivity. This means creating an environment where all team members feel valued and understood, one which welcomes diversity of thought and background. It's about creating spaces where ethical conduct is the norm, and where every individual is encouraged to contribute to their fullest potential. This type of culture not only enhances team cohesion but also elevates the entire organization's performance.

The responsibility of leadership involves making decisions which transcend the immediate benefits to the team or organization, considering the broader impact on the industry and society. Leaders must weigh the long-term consequences of their actions, ensuring their choices contribute positively to the development of the field of leadership. This approach involves considering how decisions affect all stakeholders, including employees, customers, community members, and even competitors.

Effective leaders understand their influence reaches far beyond the boardroom or office. They recognize their actions set precedents and their leadership style can inspire future generations. By embracing responsible practices, leaders not only enhance their own reputation but also contribute to the advancement of ethical leadership as a whole.

Navigating the responsibility of leadership is about much more than simply managing a team or running an organization. It's about embodying the values of stewardship, integrity, and inclusivity in every decision and action. Just as a pilot must consider the safety and well-being of every passenger and the impact of their flight on the environment, so must a leader consider the wellbeing of their team and the broader effects of their leadership. It's a comprehensive duty that demands vigilance, wisdom, and an unwavering commitment to doing what is right, not just what is expedient.

Eco-Friendly Flight Paths: Sustainability in Leadership

In aviation, choosing eco-friendly flight paths is about minimizing environmental impact.

Similarly, sustainable leadership practices ensure our methods are viable for the long haul, not depleting the resources—be it human, financial, or natural— which we depend on. It's about leading in a way that is not only effective today but also lays the foundation for future leaders to thrive.

In the aviation industry, choosing eco-friendly flight paths involves careful planning to minimize fuel consumption and reduce carbon emissions, which not only protects the environment but also improves operational efficiency. Similarly, sustainable leadership involves making decisions that consider the long-term welfare of the organization and its people. This means adopting practices which are not only effective but also judicious in their use of resources, ensuring they are not depleted for future generations.

Sustainable leadership deeply values human resources and recognizing the team's well-being is crucial for long-term success. It involves implementing policies and practices which promote work-life balance, professional development, and mental health. By investing in the growth and well-being of employees, leaders build a more resilient and motivated workforce, ready to face future challenges.

Just as eco-friendly flight paths aim to optimize fuel use, sustainable leadership practices ensure financial resources are managed wisely. This involves strategic budgeting, investing in areas which yield long-term benefits, and avoiding wasteful expenditures. Financial sustainability not only secures the organization's future but also builds trust and stability within the team.

Sustainable leadership also extends to environmental stewardship. Leaders must consider the ecological impact of their business operations and strive to reduce their carbon footprint. This can involve simple steps like reducing waste and energy consumption or more significant measures such as integrating sustainable materials and technologies into product development and manufacturing processes.

One of the primary goals of sustainable leadership is to pave the way for future generations. This means creating a framework within which new leaders can thrive—an environment rich with opportunities for innovation, supported by robust ethical practices, and guided by a clear, forwardthinking vision. Sustainable leaders not only aim to achieve success in their tenure but also to leave a legacy which empowers future leaders to build upon.

Sustainable leadership ensures the profession remains a beacon of innovation, resilience, and ethical integrity. By adopting and promoting sustainable practices, leaders not only enhance their current operations but also contribute to the health and success of the broader community and environment. Just as eco-friendly flight paths represent a commitment to the planet, sustainable leadership embodies a commitment to the future of the profession and society at large.

Maintenance and Upgrades: Continuous Improvement

Just as aircraft require regular maintenance and timely upgrades to remain operational and safe, the field of leadership demands continuous improvement and adaptation to stay relevant and effective. These parallels underscore the critical need for leaders to commit to their own

development and to foster a culture of progress within their organizations.

For leaders, continuous improvement is rooted in a personal commitment to ongoing education and professional growth. This might involve pursuing advanced degrees, attending workshops and seminars, or engaging with the latest leadership literature. Staying abreast of new theories and practices not only enhances a leader's skill set but also prepares them to navigate the complexities of modern organizational environments more effectively.

Beyond personal development, fostering an environment where innovation thrives is crucial. This means encouraging teams to propose and experiment with new ideas, approaches, and technologies. Like engineers seeking to enhance aircraft performance, leaders should seek to optimize their teams' efficiency and creativity. By valuing and integrating these innovations, organizations can remain at the forefront of their industries.

A key aspect of continuous improvement is being open to feedback. Just as pilots must heed the information from flight instruments to adjust their course, leaders must listen to feedback from their teams and peers. This feedback is invaluable for refining strategies, correcting courses, and developing leadership practices. Embracing a feedback-rich culture ensures leadership methods are not only based on past successes but are continually refined to address new challenges.

The willingness to adapt is fundamental to continuous improvement. Leadership strategies which were effective a decade ago may not yield the same results today due to changes in market dynamics, workforce expectations, and technological advancements. Leaders must be flexible, willing to discard outdated practices, and embrace new methodologies. This adaptability is crucial for ensuring the profession evolves to meet current and future challenges effectively.

The concept of maintenance and upgrades in aviation serves as a perfect analogy for continuous improvement in leadership. Regular updates, whether to software or strategy, along with routine checks and balances, help ensure that both aircraft and leadership practices operate at peak efficiency. Leaders who commit to this philosophy of continuous improvement not only enhance their own capabilities but also contribute to the long-term success and sustainability of their organizations.

Flight Training: Mentoring Future Leaders

Mentorship in leadership, akin to flight training in aviation, is a vital component in the development of capable, ethical, and innovative leaders. Just as seasoned pilots are essential for training novice aviators, experienced leaders carry the responsibility of nurturing the next generation of leadership talent. This process is not merely about the transfer of knowledge; it's a foundational strategy for ensuring the sustainability and integrity of leadership practices over time.

Mentoring future leaders involves more than imparting technical skills or sharing strategies for navigating corporate landscapes. It's about fostering a deep understanding of the values and principles which constitute effective and ethical leadership. Experienced leaders act as mentors by providing guidance, support, and insight, which help budding leaders to grow within their professional journeys and prepare them to handle future challenges.

Effective mentorship establishes a strong foundation for the future of leadership by ensuring emerging leaders are well-prepared to take on leadership roles. This preparation is comprehensive, encompassing critical thinking, ethical decision-making, and strategic planning skills. Mentors help protégés to understand complex organizational dynamics, encouraging them to think critically about their approach to leadership and the impact of their decisions.

Perhaps the most significant aspect of mentorship is the transmission of core values and principles. Experienced leaders have a unique opportunity to instill ideals such as integrity, accountability, and inclusiveness in their mentees. By modeling these values in their own behaviors and decision-making processes, mentors help to shape the ethical contours of the next leadership generation, ensuring these foundational principles continue to guide future practices.

A mentor provides continual support and guidance, offering a safety net as emerging leaders navigate their first significant challenges. This support might come in the form of advice during critical projects, feedback on leadership techniques, or help in expanding professional networks. Just as flight instructors ensure novice pilots have the support/coaching they need to handle complex flying conditions safely; leadership mentors ensure emerging leaders are never without guidance.

Mentoring in leadership, much like flight training, is crucial for the development of skilled, principled, and prepared leaders. It ensures the profession of leadership remains robust and respected and the future of leadership is characterized by a deep commitment to ethical practices and innovative approaches. Through mentorship, experienced leaders can pass on their wisdom and experience, fostering a new generation of leaders who are ready to navigate the complexities of the modern world with competence and integrity.

The Flight Deck: A Collaborative Effort

Leadership, much like navigating an aircraft, is inherently a collaborative endeavor. It thrives on the collective efforts of diverse individuals who bring their unique expertise and perspectives to the table. Just as the flight deck crew—pilots, copilots, and navigators—must work in harmony to ensure the safety and efficiency of a flight, leaders across various sectors must collaborate to advance the profession and achieve common goals.

In the vast and complex world of leadership, challenges are multifaceted and require a variety of skills and knowledge to overcome. Leaders can benefit greatly from collaborating across industries and disciplines. This cross-pollination of ideas and experiences enrich each leader's understanding and approach, leading to more innovative and effective solutions. By sharing insights, leaders can collectively address common challenges more efficiently and with greater success.

Just as each member of a flight deck contributes to navigating and operating the aircraft, each leader contributes to the resilience and success of their organizations. When leaders share their challenges and successes, they provide valuable case studies and lessons which can elevate the entire profession. This shared knowledge base becomes a powerful tool for all leaders seeking to enhance their strategies and impact.

The flight deck functions best when each team member performs their role expertly but also communicates effectively with the rest of the crew. Similarly, leadership requires a blend of diverse perspectives to ensure decisions are well-rounded and considerate of various stakeholder needs. Collaboration among leaders from different cultural, geographical, and professional backgrounds can bring new insights which challenge conventional thinking and lead to breakthrough innovations.

Creating a culture where leaders support one another and learn from each other's experiences is akin to how flight crews rely on each other's expertise and vigilance. This culture not only helps in navigating current leadership challenges but also prepares the next generation of leaders by providing them with a rich learning environment. This approach ensures the profession remains robust and capable of adapting to future challenges.

The stewardship of the leadership profession is a collective effort which mirrors the collaborative environment of an aircraft's flight deck. By working together, sharing knowledge, and supporting one another, leaders can ensure their profession remains dynamic, respected, and effective. This collective effort not only helps individual leaders to succeed but also ensures the broader field of leadership continues to thrive and adapt in an ever-changing world.

Stewardship: The Legacy of Leadership

A legacy enriched with integrity is foundational to effective leadership. This means consistently making decisions which are not only effective but are also ethical and fair. Leaders who prioritize integrity inspire trust and loyalty, creating an environment where ethical practices are the norm, and where transparency and honesty in communication and actions are valued highly.

Innovation is another cornerstone of a strong leadership legacy. Leaving a legacy of innovation involves pushing the boundaries of what is possible, encouraging creative problem-solving, and implementing forward-thinking strategies. It's about leaving the profession equipped with new tools, ideas, and approaches which enable the next generation of leaders to address future challenges more effectively.

Inspiration is a powerful legacy to leave behind. A truly impactful leader not only achieves great things but also motivates others to do the same. This involves mentoring emerging leaders, sharing insights and experiences which ignite passion, and demonstrating leadership styles which others aspire to emulate. By inspiring others, leaders ensure their influence extends far beyond their direct actions, contributing to a vibrant, dynamic future for the profession.

Ultimately, stewardship is about preparing the profession for those who will follow. This means cultivating a leadership landscape which is ready for the next generation to take it to new heights— ensuring the field remains robust, adaptable, and aligned with evolving societal and global needs. As we fly an approach in our respective leadership roles, the legacy we aim to leave should reflect our deepest values and highest aspirations. It should be a legacy which not only marks our achievements but also enhances the fabric of the leadership profession. By focusing on integrity, innovation, and inspiration, we pave the way for a future where the next generation of leaders can thrive and propel the profession to even greater heights.

Your Flight Plan: A Personal Commitment

Consider what stewardship in leadership means to you personally. How will you contribute to the sustainability, growth, and ethical foundation of the profession? Create your flight plan with intentional actions which reflect your commitment to stewardship, whether it's through mentorship, advocacy for ethical practices, or continuous personal development.

> *"Push yourself, because no one else is going to do it for you."*
>
> **- Unknown**

As we taxi to the gate, remember that the stewardship of the leadership profession is a neverending journey. It's a continuous commitment to excellence, ethics, and evolution. The choices we make today shape the trajectory of leadership for years to come.

Thank you for joining me on this flight. As we disembark, carry forward the responsibility of stewardship with pride and purpose. The future of leadership is in our hands, and together, we can ensure it soars to new, unprecedented heights.

Safe travels, fellow leaders. Until our next journey, keep your compass set on stewardship, your altitude high on integrity, and your course true to the legacy you wish to leave. The skies of leadership are vast and filled with opportunity—let's navigate them with care, commitment, and collaboration.

Chapter 14

Navigating The Skies Of Leadership: The Weight Of Command

Leadership, much like piloting, entails a profound responsibility— not just to those immediately present but also to the broader scope of the profession and community. Just as a pilot is entrusted with the lives of passengers, the integrity of the aircraft, and the vast expanses it traverses, a leader bears significant responsibilities that extend beyond day-to-day management.

The stewardship of leadership involves a deepseated commitment to uphold and foster the essence and integrity of the role. This commitment requires adhering to ethical conduct, which forms the bedrock of trust and respect within any successful organization. Ethical leadership ensures decisions and actions are not only effective but also morally sound, setting a standard for everyone within the organization to follow.

Moreover, effective stewardship in leadership demands a dedication to perpetual learning. The landscape of business and societal norms is constantly evolving, and so must the skills and knowledge of a leader. Continuous education, whether through formal training, self-directed learning, or experiential insights, is crucial for staying relevant and effective. This ongoing growth enables leaders to navigate the complexities of their roles with greater foresight and adaptability.

Nurturing an environment steeped in integrity, respect, and inclusiveness is another critical aspect of leadership stewardship. This involves creating a culture where diverse perspectives are valued and where every team member feels respected and included. An inclusive environment not only enhances team cohesion but also drives innovation, as different viewpoints often lead to unique solutions to complex problems.

Leaders must chart a course which uplifts not just their immediate team or organization but also contributes positively to the broader landscape of leadership. This means implementing practices which promote sustainability, community engagement, and the well-being of all stakeholders. By doing so, leaders can ensure their impact extends beyond the immediate operational goals to influence the industry and community in positive ways.

The responsibilities of a leader are expansive and multi-faceted, akin to those of a pilot navigating through ever-changing skies. By embracing ethical conduct, committing to continuous learning, fostering an inclusive environment, and aiming to positively influence the broader field, leaders can ensure their stewardship leaves a lasting, beneficial imprint on the horizon of leadership. This holistic approach not only enhances immediate organizational outcomes but also contributes to the shaping of an ethical, dynamic future for the leadership profession.

Throughout my tenure as a senior instructor and officer, I've encountered what can best be described as leadership turbulence— challenging moments which tested my resolve and decisionmaking acuity. Just as a pilot might face unexpected atmospheric disturbances, leaders often encounter situations where directives from higherups seem at odds with the collective wisdom of their teams.

These challenging moments often feel akin to navigating through a storm cloud, where the pressure to maintain the designated course clashes with rising dissent within the ranks. It's in these times where the true mettle of a leader is tested— not just in adhering to the path laid out by superiors but in addressing the concerns and insights of the team.

Navigating these headwinds required what I refer to as 'real talk'— open, honest communication both up the chain of command and down to the team. This approach wasn't about blind conformity to higher orders, nor was it about recklessly championing every team sentiment. Instead, it was about striking a delicate balance—

respecting and executing higher directives while also valuing and integrating the team's feedback to enhance outcomes.

My guiding principle through these turbulent times has always been a steadfast adherence to core values. Even when directives seemed misaligned with our operational ethos, it was crucial to find a way to remain true to these principles. This ofteninvolved nuanced negotiation—adhering to orders while subtly weaving in our team's insights to forge a more effective path forward.

The magic happened in the space between strict compliance and innovative adaptation. Through real conversations, where listening was as important as speaking, we fostered an environment of mutual respect. This respect was not merely given but earned, creating a dynamic where even in disagreement, every voice was valued. These discussions weren't always easy, but they were necessary for navigating the complexities of leadership and operational execution.

By balancing these dynamics—command directives with team wisdom, adherence to rules with creative input— we often hit our operational marks. This approach didn't just solve immediate problems; it also built a stronger, more cohesive team.

We learned that through genuine dialogue and mutual respect, even the most challenging leadership turbulence could be navigated successfully.

Leading through turbulence requires more than just steadfastness; it demands agility, open communication, and a deep commitment to core values. Like a skilled pilot adjusting to changing winds while keeping an eye on the destination, a leader must constantly adapt strategies, engage in meaningful dialogue, and maintain ethical standards. This dynamic approach ensures that despite the pressures and challenges, the journey forward is as successful as it is enriching for everyone involved.

And hey, let's not gloss over those not-so-smooth flights. Like that old Chinese saying goes, it's the tough times that teach you the most:

> *"Judgment comes from experience, and great judgment comes from a bad experience."*
>
> **- unknown**

In my experiences leading teams, I've found that the most turbulent rides often yield the richest gold mines of learning. True leadership isn't always about steering clear of rough weather; sometimes, it requires us to fly right through it. This approach isn't about courting trouble, but about forging a stronger, more cohesive team, ready to face whatever challenges come next.

The metaphorical bumpy rides we encounter in leadership are invaluable for growth and team building. Rather than dodging these challenges, embracing them can teach us resilience and adaptability. It's not in my job description to avoid the tough stuff. On the contrary, navigating through these difficulties is precisely my role. Each challenging situation tests our resolve and pushes us to innovate and collaborate more effectively, ultimately strengthening our team's dynamic.

Being a leader involves much more than setting the course; it requires stewardship of the values and virtues which epitomize exemplary leadership. In the expansive skies of our professional journeys, fully embracing our role as leaders means recognizing every trip—especially the challenging ones—presents an opportunity to enhance mutual understanding, foster unity, and continually aim higher.

Each difficult journey offers a unique chance to deepen our understanding of one another, to align our efforts, and to reinforce our commitment to common goals. It's about more than just surviving the storm; it's about emerging from it with a clearer sense of purpose and a stronger bond. This unity is crucial as it transforms a group of individuals into a formidable team, equipped to tackle future challenges with confidence.

A key lesson in leadership resilience is the journey doesn't end with a loss; it ends only when you quit. This philosophy underpins effective leadership—maintaining course despite setbacks, learning from every failure, and continuously striving for improvement. Leaders must exemplify this perseverance, taking the flight lead and showing by example how to navigate through adversity.

Effective leadership is characterized by the courage to face tough challenges head-on and the wisdom to see these challenges as opportunities for growth and team strengthening. It's about stewardship over the collective journey, guided by principles which foster resilience, unity, and an aspirational mindset. In the vast expanse of leadership responsibilities, every difficult journey is a step toward greater understanding and higher achievement for the entire team.

Chapter 15

Epilogue: Navigating The Leadership Skies - A Concluding Voyage

As we prepare to close the chapters of this exploration into leadership, integrating the ethos of an effective instructor with the heart of a dedicated leader, we find ourselves reflecting on the journey we've undertaken together. From the initial takeoff, soaring through the vast skies of leadership theories and practices, to embracing the role of an instructor guiding a team through uncharted territories, our voyage has been both enlightening and transformative.

The Essence of Leadership: A Continuous Learning Journey

Leadership, at its heart, is an endless journey of learning, growth, and adaptation. It's about connecting deeply with people, inspiring teams, and guiding them toward shared goals and visions. This journey is not merely about managing tasks or systems but about fostering relationships and building communities within the workplace.

Just as a pilot must master the intricacies of flight—navigating through turbulence and ensuring the safety of all passengers—a leader must develop a deep understanding of the human elements of their role. This involves more than technical skills or strategic acumen; it requires emotional intelligence, empathy, and the ability to connect with others on a meaningful level. These skills enable leaders to motivate and unite their teams, creating an environment where shared visions can be realized.

Leadership demands a commitment to lifelong learning. The landscape of business and human interaction is ever-evolving, with new challenges and opportunities continually arising. Leaders must stay at the forefront of change, not only by keeping up with industry trends and technological advancements but also by remaining attuned to the needs and aspirations of their team members. This adaptability is crucial for navigating the complex dynamics of modern organizations and markets.

While management focuses on systems, processes, and efficiency, leadership is fundamentally about people. The essence of leadership lies in the ability to connect with people, understand their motivations, and harness their collective energy towards achieving common goals. This contrasts with management, which often centers on optimizing resources, streamlining operations, and controlling outcomes. Effective leaders transcend these managerial aspects to focus on developing potential, inspiring excellence, and cultivating a culture of trust and respect.

An integral part of the leadership journey is mentorship. Leaders not only learn for their own development but also pass on their knowledge and wisdom to others. By mentoring emerging talents, experienced leaders ensure the next generation is prepared to carry forward the legacy of insightful and empathetic leadership. This cycle of teaching and learning solidifies the foundation of a robust leadership culture within any organization.

The journey of leadership is one of continuous learning and human connection. It involves a perpetual cycle of self-improvement, team engagement, and mentorship. Leaders who embrace this journey are well-equipped to inspire their teams and guide them through complexities with confidence and clarity. By focusing on the human elements of leadership rather than solely on systems and processes, leaders can create more meaningful and sustainable impacts in their organizations and industries.

Adapting to the Winds of Change: The Agile Leader

In the dynamic and often unpredictable skies of leadership, the ability to adapt swiftly and effectively to changing conditions is crucial. Like a seasoned pilot navigating through shifting winds, a skilled leader must be able to guide their team through the uncertainties of the business world with confidence and poise.

The business landscape is perpetually evolving, with new challenges and opportunities emerging at every turn. Effective leaders recognize flexibility in strategy and approach is not optional, it's essential. The ability to adapt to these changes with grace— responding to market shifts, technological advancements, and internal team dynamics—is what distinguishes a true leader from a mere manager.

While the capacity to adapt is critical, it must be balanced with the ability to maintain a steady hand. This involves guiding the team with a clear vision, even when the path to the destination shifts unexpectedly. A leader's steadiness provides the team with the confidence and security needed to venture into new territories or tackle emerging challenges without fear.

Adaptability in leadership also means having the foresight to develop strategies which are both flexible and responsive. It's about anticipating potential changes and preparing multiple pathways to success. This agility allows leaders to pivot quickly and efficiently without losing sight of the organization's core values and long-term objectives.

Despite the necessity for flexibility, all adaptations must align with the core values and objectives of the team and organization. This alignment ensures even the most significant strategic shifts contribute positively to the overall mission and vision of the organization. Leaders must weave these values into the decision-making process, ensuring each new direction not only responds to immediate challenges but also reinforces the foundational principles of the organization.

Adapting to the winds of change is an art which requires both flexibility and a firm commitment to core values. Leaders who master this balance can navigate their teams through uncertainties with assurance and agility. By remaining responsive to the ever-changing business environment while steadfastly upholding their core principles, leaders can ensure sustained success and integrity in their endeavors, no matter how turbulent the skies may become.

Cultivating a Culture of Trust and Safety: The Foundation of innovative leadership

Creating an environment where team members feel valued, understood, and supported is fundamental for fostering a thriving workplace. This atmosphere encourages innovation, creativity, and a deep sense of belonging—qualities essential for long-term organizational success. Just as an effective instructor nurtures a safe learning space, leaders must also strive to establish a culture of trust and psychological safety.

Psychological safety in the workplace means creating a setting where team members feel secure enough to express ideas, ask questions, and voice concerns without fear of ridicule or retribution. This concept is crucial in cultivating an environment where innovation can flourish. When employees feel safe, they are more likely to take risks, propose new ideas, and communicate openly, driving creativity and innovation forward.

Trust is the cornerstone of psychological safety. Leaders build trust by being transparent, consistent, and fair in their interactions and decisions. It involves showing genuine interest in the well-being and development of team members, actively listening to their input, and valuing their contributions. This trust fosters a collaborative atmosphere where challenges are tackled with collective resilience and determination.

A notable example of this in practice is the Pixar Braintrust, implemented by Ed Catmull, a cofounder of Pixar Animation Studios. The Braintrust is a group of creatives who come together during various stages of a project to review progress and provide candid feedback. This system thrives on principles of equality—everyone's input is valued equally, and there are no consequences for speaking out.

The success of this approach is evident in the consistent quality and innovation seen in Pixar's outputs, proving a culture rooted in trust and safety can lead to remarkable achievements.

Leaders must encourage open communication and show it is okay to fail. This attitude helps to eliminate fear associated with taking risks and innovations. By promoting a mindset where failure is seen as a learning opportunity rather than a setback, leaders can enhance their team's resilience and adaptability.

Cultivating a culture of trust and psychological safety is akin to nurturing a garden. It requires patience, care, and consistent effort. Leaders who invest in these areas reap the benefits of a more engaged, innovative, and collaborative workforce.

By ensuring every team member feels secure and valued, leaders not only enhance individual and team performance but also contribute to the development of a dynamic and inclusive organizational culture.

Engaging the Heart and Mind

Engagement and motivation are the fuel which propels the team forward. Effective leaders recognize the power of connecting with team members not just professionally but also on a personal level. By understanding their passions, strengths, and aspirations, leaders can unlock the full potential of their teams, driving performance and satisfaction simultaneously.

The first step in engaging both the heart and mind is to truly understand the individuals who make up the team. This means going beyond surface-level interactions and getting to know them as people with unique backgrounds, interests, and career goals. Leaders can conduct regular one-onone meetings, foster an open communication environment, and use empathetic listening to really hear what their team members are passionate about and what drives them.

Once leaders understand their team members' personal and professional motivations, they can begin to align these with the organization's broader mission. It's about igniting a shared passion which transcends day-to-day tasks and galvanizes the team toward a common goal. This alignment not only boosts morale but also enhances productivity, as team members feel more connected to the work they are doing and understand how it contributes to the larger objectives.

Beyond alignment, creating a sense of purpose is crucial. When team members see their work has meaning and impact, they are more likely to put in extra effort and remain committed even in challenging times. Leaders can foster this sense of purpose by highlighting the significance of the team's achievements, celebrating milestones, and demonstrating how each role within the team contributes to the overall success of the organization.

Successful engagement requires both emotional and intellectual buy-in. Leaders should strive to appeal to the emotions by crafting a narrative around the team's mission which resonates on a personal level. At the same time, they must engage their intellect by setting clear, achievable goals and providing the resources needed to attain them. This dual approach ensures team members are not only emotionally invested in their work but also equipped to succeed.

Engaging both the hearts and minds of team members is a powerful strategy which fosters a robust, motivated, and cohesive team. Leaders who excel in this are able to tap into the full range of human potential, driving their teams to perform at their best and find deep satisfaction in their work. This holistic approach to leadership not only enhances individual and team performance but also builds a resilient, passionate workforce committed to achieving shared goals.

The Power of Feedback and Reflection: Navigating Towards Continuous Improvement

In the dynamic realm of leadership, akin to navigating a flight, continuous improvement for both the leader and their team is crucially fueled by constructive feedback and reflective practice. Just as pilots must constantly adjust their course based on real-time feedback from their instruments and environment, leaders must similarly guide their teams with precision and foresight, leveraging feedback and reflection to enhance performance and trajectory.

Leaders, much like coaches, play a pivotal role in providing guidance and support while fostering an environment ripe for growth and learning. This involves not only directing the team towards immediate objectives but also preparing them for future challenges and successes. By actively engaging in coaching, leaders help team members develop essential skills and competencies, encouraging them to take initiative and responsibility for their personal and professional growth.

Constructive feedback is the radar which helps navigate the often- turbulent skies of workplace dynamics. It involves clear, specific, and actionable insights which team members can use to adjust their performance. Effective leaders ensure feedback is delivered in a manner which is supportive and empowering, rather than critical or demoralizing, facilitating a culture where continuous improvement is both encouraged and celebrated.

Reflective practice is akin to a pilot reviewing a flight's path after landing—it involves looking back at the journey to understand what went well and what could be improved. Leaders must regularly reflect not only on their own leadership practices but also on the team's overall performance and dynamics. This reflection helps in learning from both successes and setbacks, ensuring that future decisions and actions are informed by past experiences and accumulated wisdom.

Just as a pilot learns from every flight, leaders and their teams must learn from every project, meeting, and interaction. This continuous loop of performing, reflecting, and adjusting ensures the path forward is increasingly informed and refined. Reflection allows leaders to consider the broader implications of their actions, adapt their strategies, and better align their goals with their team's capabilities and aspirations.

The power of feedback and reflection in leadership is instrumental in steering both the leader and their team towards continual improvement and success. By embracing the roles of a coach and reflective practitioner, leaders can ensure that their teams are not only performing optimally but are also prepared for future challenges. This ongoing process of navigation and adjustment, much like piloting through shifting skies, is essential for maintaining course and reaching new heights of achievement.

Until we meet again, shoot for the stars.

Chapter 16

Preparing For Descent And Final Approach

The phases of preparing for a descent into the terminal area and finalizing the approach in aviation offer rich parallels to strategic business planning and execution as projects or initiatives near their culmination. These moments in a flight require pilots to transition from cruising altitude to a more engaged and detailed focus on the tasks required for a safe and successful landing. It's about adjusting from the broad view to a finer, more precise one, preparing meticulously for what's to come.

In the business realm, this corresponds to the critical phase of wrapping up a project or steering a strategy towards its intended outcomes. Just as a pilot starts to consider altitude adjustments, speed reductions, and the sequence of actions needed for landing, a leader must shift focus towards ensuring that all elements of the project are aligned for a smooth completion. It involves reviewing the project's objectives, ensuring that all tasks are on track, and that the team is prepared for the final push.

The preparation for descent in business also means tightening up on details that might have been broader strokes at higher altitudes. It's about finetuning, making sure that all the pieces fit together perfectly, and preparing for any adjustments that need to be made before the project lands. This might involve final stakeholder communications, last-minute quality checks, or aligning resources for the final steps.

The Approach: Setting Your Sights on New Horizons

As we begin our approach, it's vital to reflect on the journey thus far while setting our sights on new horizons. Leadership, much like piloting, is about constantly scanning the environment, anticipating changes, and being prepared for the next adventure. As we navigate the airways of leadership and strategy, a reminder rings clear and compelling: we are now on our final approach, with the runway firmly within our sights. This moment, when the pilot aligns the aircraft with its final approach path, serves as a critical juncture not only in aviation but in every business venture we undertake.

Let me underscore this point with all the gravity it commands: while our eyes naturally shift towards the horizon, eager to embark on the next chapter, our immediate priority must be to ensure the successful closure of our current endeavor. This phase, the careful and deliberate completion of what we've set in motion, is what ultimately propels us forward, laying the groundwork for future success.

The allure of the "next big thing" is undeniable. Foresight and the anticipation of leading another project or venture are not just exciting but essential traits of a visionary leader. Yet, in this eagerness to advance, there lies a perilous trap—the potential to overlook or undervalue the critical closing stages of our present journey.

It is in these concluding moments that our focus is tested most. The completion of a project, much like the safe landing of an aircraft, requires undivided attention to detail, a commitment to excellence, and a disciplined adherence to the processes that ensure a successful outcome. It's a reminder of the brilliance of a journey not only in its launch or in the heights it reaches but equally in how gracefully and effectively it concludes.

In business, as in aviation, the final approach and landing are not mere formalities but pivotal moments demanding precision, calm, and foresight. This is the culmination of all the planning, effort, and dedication invested in the venture. Successfully navigating this phase solidifies achievements, consolidates gains, and sets the stage for future endeavors.

Therefore, as we line up with our runway, let's embrace the discipline to see through the current venture with as much enthusiasm and rigor as we plan for the next. It's a balanced approach which ensures not only the success of our immediate project but also fortifies our trajectory towards future ventures. In a number of instances, the enthusiasm and rigor for the next venture is multiplied and the effects of success become desired even more.

What new destinations await your leadership? How will you chart the course to unexplored territories? Like a pilot reviewing the flight plan, assess your leadership path and prepare for the next journey with enthusiasm and purpose.

Final Approach: Looking Ahead

As we begin our descent in this conversation, remember the journey of leadership, much like flying, is an ongoing learning experience. There will always be new skies to explore, new challenges to navigate, and new destinations to reach.

Final approach preparation in aviation is not just about the plane and its passengers but also about ensuring that the conditions at the airport are right for landing.

Similarly, in business, this phase is about creating the right conditions for the project or initiative's completion. This means ensuring that the organizational environment is prepared for the integration of the project's results, that stakeholders are informed and aligned, and that any potential obstacles to successful completion have been identified and mitigated.

This detailed, focused preparation is crucial for ensuring a smooth transition from project execution to project completion and integration. It ensures that, much like a well-executed landing, the project achieves its goals with minimal disruption and maximum impact.

By drawing from the careful, focused approach required in aviation as pilots prepare for descent and approach, business leaders can ensure their projects are guided to successful completion with the same level of precision and readiness.

This analogy underscores the importance of shifting from the broad strategies employed at cruising altitude to the detailed, tactical planning necessary for a successful landing.

Thank you for embarking on this flight of exploration and discovery in leadership. May your journey be filled with clear skies, favorable winds, and remarkable vistas. And when you encounter turbulence, may you navigate it with grace, leading your team to new heights of success and fulfillment.

Until our paths cross again in the endless sky of leadership, keep your altimeter set on your goals, your eyes on the horizon, and your heart open to the journey. The sky is vast, and the possibilities are endless. Here's to the adventure of leadership and the uncharted territories we'll explore together.

Tailwinds and clear skies, my fellow aviator. The journey continues, and I can't wait to see where it takes us next.

Chapter 17

Landing Gear Down: The Grace Of Concluding Chapters

Just as every flight must eventually touch down, bringing our aerial journey of leadership to a graceful landing is an art. It's about knowing when it's time to descend, making the necessary preparations, and ensuring a smooth flare and touchdown leaving everyone feeling accomplished and ready for the next takeoff…passengers included.

Safe Landings: Celebrating Successes

Think of every smooth landing after a long flight— the relief, the satisfaction, and yes, the celebration that comes with it. It's the same vibe when you wrap up a big project or hit a major goal in the business world. It's not just another item checked off the list; it's a milestone, a moment that deserves a highfive, a pat on the back, or maybe even a round of applause.

Yes, this is a repeat of being the Chief Encouragement Officer/Head Cheerleader. The subject is coming up again to highlight just how important it is for your team to know that you not only recognize all that they do, but you are also more willing than anyone else to celebrate the achievements openly. Taking the time to really recognize the hustle and heart your team has put in is like throwing a mini party for every success. It's about saying, "Hey, we did this together, and it's pretty awesome." These celebrations do more than just make people feel good (though that's super important too). They're like fuel for the team's spirit, making everyone pumped and ready for the next big challenge.

Imagine ending a successful project with nothing but a nod. Now, the picture ends with some genuine thanks, maybe some treats or a gift card, how about a weekend getaway? The point is you are providing the team with a real moment of appreciation for the hard work everyone's put in. The difference is night and day, right? Celebrating successes, big or small, reinforces the bond within the team and highlights the value of their efforts. It's these moments of recognition that remind everyone why they're part of the team and why their contributions matter.

Ground Taxi: Leaving the runway!

Similarly, after a project's "flight," the ground taxi phase is crucial for ensuring a smooth transition to regular operations or the next big project. It's about taking the time to analyze outcomes, celebrate successes, gather feedback, and incorporate insights into future planning. This phase ensures that the momentum of success is harnessed and that any lessons from missteps are learned.

The parallels between ground taxiing in aviation and strategic planning and debriefing in business highlight the importance of careful preparation and reflective learning. Both require a detailed understanding of the current environment, a clear vision of the destination, and a plan for navigating the path between. In both realms, success is not only about the journey in the air but also about how effectively one manages the transitions before takeoff and after landing.

By drawing from the discipline and precision required in aviation's ground taxiing, business leaders can appreciate the value of thorough planning and effective debriefing. These stages frame the main event, ensuring that every project or initiative is set up for success and that every lesson is captured for continuous improvement.

Crew Debrief: Learning from the Flight

In the aviation world, conducting a debrief is an essential tool for safety and efficiency, a practice meticulously adopted by the military, FAA, pilots, and their crews after each flight. This methodology, when applied to the business landscape, becomes an invaluable strategy for navigating the complexities and challenges of the corporate world.

Imagine your team as the crew of a high-stakes flight, where the business projects and initiatives you take on a life which is diverse and often laced with turbulent journeys. Each project completion or milestone achieved offers a unique opportunity for a debrief, a moment to collectively pause and reflect on the voyage from inception to realization.

The debrief in a business context goes beyond a mere review meeting. It is an intentional dialogue where successes are dissected to understand the underlying factors which can be replicated in future endeavors. Additionally, it is a forum where mistakes/missteps are analyzed not with a view to establish blame, but with the aim of gleaning insights capable of steering future strategies away from similar pitfalls.

This reflective exercise is especially critical in the fast-evolving business landscape, where adaptability and continuous improvement are not just desirable attributes but are essential survival skills. By institutionalizing debriefs as a part of your team's culture, you create a resilient framework which encourages learning from every outcome— be it a triumphant success or a humbling setback.

Moreover, in the business realm, where projects often involve cross-functional teams and stakeholders with varying perspectives and interests, debrief sessions serve as a crucial platform for fostering unity and alignment. They allow for a holistic view of the project's impact, integrating feedback from diverse quarters and ensuring that every member's contribution is acknowledged and learned from.

The practice of debriefing also significantly contributes to building a culture of transparency and trust within the organization. By openly discussing what worked, what didn't, and how to improve, leaders model accountability and openness, setting a precedent that encourages honesty and constructive feedback among all team members.

Incorporating debriefs into the rhythm of business operations thus transforms each project and task into a lesson, a step in the collective journey of growth and improvement. It's a strategy that not only enhances the effectiveness and cohesion of teams but also aligns closely with the dynamic needs and challenges of the contemporary business landscape.

Chapter 18

Maintenance Check: Self-Care And Team Care

No aircraft is sent back into the skies without a thorough maintenance check. Similarly, after significant milestones or projects, it's crucial for you and your team to recharge and rejuvenate. Leadership demands energy, creativity, and resilience, all of which are replenished through rest and self-care. Encourage your team to take time for themselves, and lead by example. A well-

maintained team, like a well-maintained aircraft, is ready for the challenges and opportunities of the next journey.

The Hangar: A Place for Reflection and Preparation

In the journey of leadership, "The Hangar" serves as a crucial metaphorical space, much like the quiet, introspective area where aircraft are stored and maintained between flights. It is here, away from the noise and demands of daily operations, where leaders can engage in deep reflection and meticulous preparation, setting the stage for future endeavors.

After each leadership "flight"—whether a project, a fiscal quarter, or a significant event—taking the time to retreat to the hangar is vital. This period of reflection allows leaders to contemplate the lessons learned from recent experiences. What strategies succeeded? What challenges were encountered? How did the team respond? Reflecting on these questions in the quiet aftermath helps leaders consolidate gains, learn from mistakes, and enhance their approach.

The hangar is also a place for measuring the distances traveled— both literally and figuratively—and acknowledging the growth experienced by the team and the leaders themselves. It provides a moment to celebrate achievements and recognize the development of skills and relationships which have taken place under the pressures and triumphs of the journey.

Moreover, the hangar is where preparation for the next launch begins. In this space, leaders can dream about new destinations and plan for upcoming adventures. This involves setting new goals, designing strategies, and aligning resources to ensure that the next phase of the journey is as prepared as possible. Preparation might include training for the team, revising protocols, or innovating new approaches to meet the challenges of the future.

Armed with insights gained from reflection, leaders can plan more effectively. They can anticipate potential issues and opportunities more accurately, ensuring when the team leaves the hangar, they are better equipped, more confident, and unified toward a common purpose. This proactive planning helps in building resilience and adaptability, key traits needed for navigating the uncertain terrains which may lie ahead.

The Hangar is not merely a pause in activity; it is an active, strategic phase in the leadership journey. It offers a unique opportunity to refine tactics, bolster morale, and fortify the team's readiness. Leaders who utilize this space effectively ensure their teams are not only recovering from the past but are also reinvigorated and inspired for the future. This reflective and preparatory phase is crucial for sustaining momentum and achieving long-term success.

The cycle of continuous leadership mirrors the perpetual cycles of flight. Each landing provides an opportunity to reflect, learn, and plan, but it is fundamentally a precursor to the next takeoff. It's a moment to catch our breath, to assess our performance, and to prepare for the challenges and opportunities which lie ahead. This cyclical process ensures leaders remain proactive, responsive, and ever-evolving.

With every new takeoff, leaders embrace the chance to pursue new dreams, goals, and adventures. This forward-looking perspective is crucial for maintaining momentum and enthusiasm within the team. It encourages a culture of aspiration and achievement, where the potential for innovation and success knows no bounds. Leaders set the pace, instilling a sense of excitement and possibility that propels the entire team forward.

Each new flight phase in leadership provides an opportunity to implement lessons learned from previous journeys. This adaptive approach allows leaders to refine their strategies, enhance their skills, and innovate in response to new information and changing conditions. Just as pilots adjust their flight paths based on weather conditions and air traffic, effective leaders modify their tactics based on market dynamics, team feedback, and other external factors.

The journey of leadership requires resilience and determination. Just as a pilot must navigate through turbulence and unforeseen challenges, leaders must be prepared to handle obstacles and setbacks without losing sight of their destination. This perseverance is key to sustaining success in the long term, ensuring each new takeoff is as focused and determined as the last.

The leadership journey, much like the journey of flight, never truly ends. Each landing is a gateway to the next takeoff—a new beginning filled with potential and promise. Leaders who embrace this continuous journey cultivates a dynamic environment where learning, growth, and innovation are ongoing. By staying clear for takeoff, leaders ensure their teams are always ready to soar to new heights, chase new dreams, and achieve new successes.

Clear for Takeoff: The Journey Never Ends

The journey of leadership is inherently dynamic and unending, akin to the continuous cycle of flight. Each phase of leadership—from decision-making and team management to strategy implementation—parallels the stages of a flight. As leaders taxi back to the runway, preparing for the next takeoff, it serves as a powerful reminder that the end of one journey marks the beginning of another.

In the world of aviation, no flight is the final one unless the pilot decides to retire the aircraft. Similarly, in leadership, each landing is merely a brief pause—a moment to reflect, regroup, and recharge before taking to the skies once again. This continuous cycle is not just about persistence but about embracing the opportunity to pursue new dreams, goals, and adventures.

These brief pauses are crucial. They provide leaders with an opportunity to catch their breath, evaluate their performance, and integrate lessons learned into future strategies. This reflective practice is essential for growth, allowing leaders to develop deeper insights into their leadership style and the needs of their team.

Take, for example, Richard Branson, a renowned entrepreneur whose career is a testament to continuous leadership and innovation. Branson has never been one to shy away from new ventures, regardless of the industry. From music to airlines, and space tourism, Branson's leadership journey exemplifies how each venture, while distinct, is part of a larger, ongoing journey of exploration and achievement. His ability to move from one industry to another—always with fresh enthusiasm and strategic focus— illustrates the concept of 'clear for takeoff' in a real-world context.

With every new takeoff, leaders have the chance to redefine their goals and set new benchmarks for success. It's about leveraging the accumulated wisdom from past experiences while remaining open to the innovations and possibilities which lie ahead. This mindset not only motivates the leader but also inspires the entire team, creating a culture of ambition and continuous improvement.

Just as a pilot views each flight as a component of a much larger career journey, leaders should view each project, each role, and each challenge as part of an ongoing journey. The key is to remain vigilant, prepared, and enthusiastic for what comes next, maintaining the momentum and passion needed to navigate the ever-evolving landscapes of leadership. The journey never ends, and for those who lead, the horizon always holds new possibilities to explore and conquer.

Your Copilot: The Importance of Mentorship in Leadership

In both the flight deck and the realm of leadership, the role of a pilot/copilot or mentor is crucial. Just as a pilot/copilot provides support, shares insights, and ensures the safety and efficiency of a flight, a mentor in leadership offers guidance, wisdom, and support, helping to navigate the often complex journey of professional growth and development. This individual(s) could be a peer, an instructor, or someone from another organization with more years of experience. The mandate is to seek out those who have navigated the path before you and be open to learning from their experiences good or bad. Likewise, offer your wing to mentor others. Leadership is a shared journey, and together, we can reach greater heights.

Having a mentor is like having a seasoned navigator by your side. Mentors, with their wealth of experience and knowledge, have already traversed similar paths and faced common challenges. By seeking out such individuals, emerging leaders can gain invaluable insights which only firsthand experience can teach. This guidance helps in making informed decisions, avoiding common pitfalls, and accelerating personal and professional growth.

Mentorship is not a one-way street; it provides profound benefits to both mentors and mentees. For mentors, the act of guiding someone else enables them to refine their leadership style, enhance their communication skills, and reaffirm their own knowledge and experiences. For mentees, it offers a trusted source of advice, a sounding board for ideas, and a reliable support system in the face of challenges.

Consider the impactful mentorship between Steve Jobs and Mark Zuckerberg. Jobs, an established innovator, and business leader, provided guidance and support to Zuckerberg during the early years of Facebook. This relationship exemplified how a seasoned leader could help a younger entrepreneur navigate complex decisions and strategic challenges, significantly impacting Zuckerberg's approach to leadership and business strategy.

Just as important as seeking mentorship is offering it to others. Experienced leaders have a responsibility to share their journey, imparting lessons learned to help nurture the next generation of leaders. By acting as mentors, seasoned professionals can give back to the community and enrich the overall culture of their industries, ensuring that the legacy of good leadership continues.

Ultimately, leadership is a shared journey. No leader succeeds in isolation. The collaborative nature of mentorship—much like the partnership between pilot and copilot—ensures knowledge is passed down, skills are honed, and both individuals grow in their respective roles. Together, through effective mentorship, leaders at all levels can reach greater heights, achieving more than they could alone.

Cultivating a culture of mentorship within organizations or communities is essential for fostering a healthy, dynamic leadership environment. Leaders should actively seek mentors and also offer themselves as mentors to others. This culture of guidance and shared experience not only enhances individual careers but also strengthens the entire organizational structure, much like a wellcoordinated flight deck leads to a successful and safe journey.

Flight Log: Recording Your Leadership Journey

In the world of aviation, a flight log is essential for tracking progress, experiences, and lessons learned during flights. Similarly, keeping a detailed record of your leadership journey serves as a powerful tool for personal and professional growth. This log acts not only as a historical record of achievements and challenges but also as a strategic guide for future endeavors.

Maintaining a leadership log involves more than simply noting down achievements or challenges; it's about reflecting on the experiences which shape you as a leader.

Recording milestones, lessons learned, and destinations reached allow you to analyze your growth over time, identify patterns in your leadership style, and refine your strategies. This log serves as a living document which not only maps out your past experiences but also sets the course for future successes.

An exemplary figure who embodies the principles of recording and reflecting on one's leadership journey is Michelle Obama. Throughout her time as the First Lady and thereafter, Michelle Obama has painstakingly captured her experiences and lessons in various forms, from speeches and interviews to her memoir, "Becoming." Her reflective practices have allowed her to share insightful leadership lessons with a global audience, inspiring many with her journey from a working-class neighborhood in Chicago to the White House.

Michelle Obama's approach to leadership highlights the importance of understanding one's journey, recognizing personal growth, and using knowledge to inspire and lead others. Her ability to articulate her experiences and the lessons she has learned are powerful examples of how leaders can use their personal journeys to influence and mentor others positively.

Your leadership log, much like a flight log, is more than just a retrospective account—it's a roadmap for your future. By regularly reviewing your log, you can assess where you need more development, which strategies have been effective, and how your actions align with your long-term goals. This ongoing process ensures your leadership practice remains dynamic, responsive, and aligned with your evolving aspirations.

Moreover, a leadership log serves as a reminder of your capabilities and the impact you've made. In moments of doubt or challenge, reviewing your past successes and the obstacles you've overcome can provide the motivation and confidence needed to face new challenges. It reaffirms your ability to lead effectively and make a significant impact.

Keeping a detailed log of your leadership journey is a critical practice for any leader seeking to maximize their potential and effectiveness. It allows leaders to remain mindful of their growth, prepare for future challenges, and continue making informed, impactful decisions. For leaders like Michelle Obama, such practices not only enhance their own leadership capacity but also serve as an invaluable legacy and source of inspiration for others following in their footsteps.

As we prepare for our next departure, let's embrace the endless sky of leadership with excitement and anticipation. The horizon is filled with limitless potential, and the skies are waiting for us to explore.

Here's to the leaders who dare to fly, to navigate the unknown, and to inspire others to spread their wings. The adventure continues, and the skies are calling.

Clear skies and favorable winds to you, my fellow leader. Let's make this journey extraordinary. Until next time, keep your eyes on the stars and your heart full of dreams. The next chapter awaits, and it's bound to be an incredible flight.

Chapter 19

Time To Instruct: Blending Leadership With Effective Instruction

Leaders as instructors not only direct tasks and manage workflows but also impart knowledge, share experiences, and cultivate skills among their team members. This dual role involves a deep understanding of the professional landscape and the ability to convey this understanding in ways which resonate and inspire. By effectively instructing their teams, leaders can ensure knowledge and best practices permeate throughout the organization, enhancing productivity and cohesion.

Incorporating the essence of instruction into leadership transcends the boundaries of traditional training by embedding continuous learning into the very fabric of the organizational culture. This approach involves a consistent commitment to educating and mentoring team members, which is pivotal not only for personal and professional development but also for attracting and retaining talented individuals.

Leaders who focus on instruction create an environment that values continuous improvement and professional growth. This can include formal training programs designed to enhance specific skills, informal coaching sessions to address immediate challenges, and everyday interactions which present opportunities for teaching moments. By fostering a learning-focused environment, organizations signal to current and prospective employees that they are committed to their development. This is particularly appealing to top talent, who often seek out environments where they can grow skills and advance their careers.

Effective leaders are adept at recognizing teaching moments in everyday tasks and interactions. These opportunities, when utilized correctly, can lead to profound learning experiences which resonate more deeply than formal training sessions. Leaders who can seamlessly integrate these lessons into daily workflows not only enhance learning but also demonstrate their commitment to their team's development. This capability to weave instruction into the fabric of daily operations shows the organization values ongoing development, a key factor in retaining talented team members.

A consistent commitment to mentoring and education helps in building a reputation as an employer that invests in its people. For talented professionals looking for places where they can thrive, such an environment is highly attractive.

They are more likely to join and stay with an organization that not only challenges them but also provides clear pathways for learning and advancement.

An inspiring example of this is found in Denzel

Washington's approach to his career in the arts, both as an accomplished actor and a mentor. Washington has been known not only for his stellar performances but also for his dedication to guiding emerging talent in the film industry. His work at the American Film Institute, where he has offered master classes, showcases his commitment to nurturing new actors. Denzel frequently emphasizes the importance of discipline, continuous learning, and the mastery of one's craft, underlining the instructional aspect of his leadership within the arts community.

When leaders like Denzel Washington teach and mentor, they do more than transfer knowledge; they inspire their mentees to pursue excellence with the same passion and dedication they exhibit. This kind of leadership builds a legacy of skill and enthusiasm that can outlast the leader's direct involvement. It creates a multiplier effect, where those mentored can themselves become mentors, perpetuating a culture of growth and learning.

Let's consider Google, renowned for its vibrant culture of innovation and learning. Google invests heavily in employee development programs, ranging from technical training to cutting-edge technologies to leadership workshops and personal growth sessions. This commitment to growth not only helps Google stay at the forefront of technological innovation but also makes it highly attractive to ambitious professionals who seek environments where they can develop new skills and take on challenging projects.

Integrating the essence of instruction into leadership is a strategic advantage which extends beyond enhancing individual and organizational capabilities. It is a key factor in attracting and retaining top talent. Organizations who prioritize continuous learning and development are seen as desirable workplaces for ambitious professionals. By cultivating an environment where learning is embedded in every aspect of the organizational culture, leaders can ensure a committed, motivated, and highly skilled workforce ready to meet future challenges even in the midst of turnover.

1. Leadership as Continuous Learning:

Embracing the role of an instructor within the sphere of leadership commands a deep-seated commitment to lifelong learning. This principle is foundational, reflecting the perpetual evolution required to remain effective and relevant in any leadership position. Just as an instructor must keep up with the latest advancements in their field, a leader must continuously expand their understanding of their industry, their team, and the broader business environment.

In today's rapidly changing world, leaders must ensure they are well informed about the latest trends, technologies, and methodologies within their industries.

This ongoing education might involve participating in professional development courses, attending industry conferences, or maintaining active memberships in relevant professional organizations. Staying updated allows leaders to anticipate changes and make informed decisions that keep their organizations competitive and innovative.

Continuous learning also extends to understanding team dynamics and the diverse needs of team members. Leaders must be students of human behavior, striving to grasp what motivates their employees, how they work best, and what challenges they face. This understanding can lead to more effective communication, better conflict resolution, and a more inclusive culture that aligns with the values and goals of the organization.

A leader's commitment to learning sets a compelling example for their team, establishing a standard for how challenges and new information are approached.

By openly engaging in learning and demonstrating their own development, leaders inspire their teams to embrace a similar mindset. This culture of curiosity and professional growth encourages employees to seek out learning opportunities, innovate, and take informed risks, which can lead to significant advancements for the entire organization.

Consider Satya Nadella, CEO of Microsoft, who has famously prioritized a "learn-it-all" culture over a "know-it-all" culture. Under his leadership, Microsoft has rejuvenated its approach to innovation and market presence, largely attributed to this cultural shift towards continuous learning and humility. Nadella's own commitment to personal and professional growth—through reading, engaging with diverse perspectives, and adapting leadership styles—has made him a paragon of modern leadership. His approach not only transformed Microsoft's corporate culture but also dramatically increased its market value.

Leadership as continuous learning is an integral practice which goes beyond mere personal development—it is a strategic approach that drives organizational success.

Leaders who commit to this ongoing educational journey not only enhance their own expertise but also foster an environment where growth, curiosity, and innovation flourish. By embodying the values of continuous learning, leaders can inspire their teams to pursue excellence, adapt to change, and achieve outstanding results.

2. Tailoring Your Approach:

Just as effective instructors adapt their teaching strategies to accommodate diverse learning styles, effective leaders tailor their leadership approach to the individual needs, strengths, and motivations of their team members. This personalized approach ensures that each team member feels valued and understood, maximizing their engagement and productivity. It requires keen observation, active listening, and the flexibility to adjust leadership styles as needed—a true mark of instructional acumen applied to leadership.

As a standardization officer in the AH-64A/D Attack Helicopter, I coached and mentored crews throughout the organizations under my purview. I learned to adapt my instruction and match it with not just the crew but the individuals who made up the crew. This provided me with the opportunity to be better, to learn, and to enhance my people skills while building effective combat teams. It forced me to find a technique to break through and reach the individual and thereby develop the crew.

> *"In order to succeed, we must first believe that we can."*
>
> **Nikos Kazantzakis**

I was then able to better develop battle teams which led to the development of premier organizations operating within the joint environment conducting theater-level operations. I was able to lean on my fellow standardization officers and together we worked to enhance the commander's ability to focus strategically.

3. Creating a Safe Environment for Growth:

In the realm of education, instructors understand the importance of a safe learning environment— one where students are encouraged to ask questions, make mistakes, and explore new ideas without fear. This principle is equally vital in leadership, where the cultivation of psychological safety within a team can significantly enhance innovation, learning, and overall team dynamics.

> *"I have not failed. I've just found 10,000 ways that won't work."*
>
> **- Thomas A. Edison**

Psychological safety is foundational for effective teamwork and innovation. It refers to an atmosphere where team members feel secure enough to be open and honest about their thoughts, challenges, and mistakes. Leaders play a crucial role in establishing this kind of environment by actively demonstrating support and understanding. When team members do not fear judgment or retribution for mistakes, they are more likely to engage in creative problem-solving, share innovative ideas, and communicate more effectively.

Leaders can foster psychological safety by encouraging open communication and creating opportunities for team members to experiment with new approaches. This might involve regular open-

forum discussions, anonymous feedback mechanisms, or structured brainstorming sessions where all ideas are welcomed and considered. By valuing diverse perspectives and encouraging exploration, leaders reinforce the message that the team's growth is a priority, and each member's contributions are valued.

An essential aspect of creating a safe environment is how mistakes are handled. Leaders should approach errors not as failures but as valuable learning opportunities. This approach involves analyzing what went wrong, discussing it openly without placing blame, and determining how to avoid similar issues in the future. When mistakes are treated as part of the learning process, it reduces fear among team members about trying new things and pushes the boundaries of what they can achieve.

A safe and supportive environment significantly strengthens trust and cohesion within a team. Trust is built when team members feel their leader is committed to their growth and success. This trust, in turn, fosters a more collaborative and supportive team dynamic, where members are motivated to support each other's efforts and success.

Just as instructors must nurture a safe learning environment to effectively educate their students, leaders must cultivate an atmosphere of psychological safety to unlock the full potential of their teams. This environment is crucial for accelerating learning, fostering innovation, and building a strong, cohesive team. Leaders who successfully create and maintain a safe space for growth ensure their teams are not only more productive and innovative but also more satisfied and engaged in their work.

4. Engaging and Motivating: The Role of a Leader-Instructor

Engagement is a fundamental element that drives both educational and workplace success. A leader, much like an instructor in a classroom, plays a pivotal role in engaging and motivating team members by making their roles meaningful and interactive. This engagement is crucial for fostering a positive work environment and driving the team towards collective and individual successes.

> *"You don't have to be great to start, but you have to start to be great."*
>
> **- Zig Ziglar**

One of the core responsibilities of a leader is to make tasks meaningful for every team member. This involves clearly connecting daily activities to the organization's broader goals. When team members understand how their work contributes to the larger objectives, they are more likely to find their tasks rewarding and engage more deeply with their responsibilities. Leaders can enhance this connection by regularly communicating the organization's vision and demonstrating how specific roles and projects advance these aims.

Recognition is a powerful motivator... have you heard this before? This cannot be stated enough, leaders who acknowledge the individual contributions of team members not only boost morale but also reinforce the value of each person's work. This recognition can be as simple as thanking a team member for their hard work in a meeting or as formal as instituting a rewards system highlighting outstanding contributions. Such recognition helps to cultivate a culture of appreciation and respect, which are key ingredients for maintaining high levels of engagement.

Incorporating team members in decision-making processes is another effective strategy to enhance engagement and motivation. By inviting input on decisions which affect their work and the broader organizational direction, leaders foster a sense of ownership among team members. This participatory approach is akin to the interactive nature of effective instruction, where students are encouraged to contribute ideas and engage in problem-solving activities. In the workplace, this might involve brainstorming sessions, strategy meetings, or feedback loops that allow employees to voice their opinions and suggestions.

When team members are actively involved in shaping the direction of their work and the organization, they naturally develop a stronger commitment to the team's success. This sense of ownership makes them more invested in the outcomes of their efforts and motivates them to go above and beyond in their roles. Leaders can foster this ownership by delegating meaningful responsibilities and supporting autonomous project management.

In the military, especially within combat arms units, competition serves as a powerful motivator. It's not uncommon to see a service member's name and rank on a piece of equipment, sparking a fierce but friendly contest. Everyone strives for their gear to be the 'King of the Mountain,' ensuring it performs flawlessly. This sense of ownership drives crew members in aviation units across all service branches. They take immense pride in their work, always eager for those bragging rights—it all starts with the motivation which comes from taking ownership.

Integrating the dynamics of effective instruction into leadership—through meaningful engagement, recognition, participatory decision-making, and fostering ownership— can significantly enhance team motivation and commitment. Leaders who adopt these instructional principles in their management practices create an environment where team members are not only motivated to achieve but are also committed to contributing to the organization's long-term success. This synergy between engagement and instruction ensures that the workplace mimics the vitality and interactive nature of the most effective learning environments.

5. Providing Feedback and Coaching:

Feedback and coaching are indispensable in the arsenal of any effective leader, mirroring the role of an instructor who guides students through their learning journey. Just as a flight instructor provides crucial guidance to pilot trainees, a leader, embracing an instructor's mindset, focuses on nurturing the growth and development of their team members through constructive feedback.

Constructive feedback is a cornerstone of effective leadership. It's not just about pointing out areas for improvement; it's about providing guidance which helps individuals build their skills and boost their performance. The best leaders, like skilled instructors, know how to deliver feedback in a way which is clear, specific, and supportive, ensuring it leads to positive changes and personal growth.

Just as a flight instructor adapts their teaching strategies to the learning style and progress of each student, effective leaders tailor their feedback and coaching to suit the unique developmental needs of each team member. This personalized approach helps foster a deep sense of engagement and respect, as team members feel valued and understood. It also maximizes the impact of feedback, as it directly addresses the individual's specific challenges and goals.

Beyond giving feedback, leaders as coaches engage in ongoing developmental dialogues that encourage continuous learning and improvement. This might involve setting performance goals, discussing career aspirations, or working through current work challenges. Effective coaching empowers individuals to reflect on their experiences, learn from their mistakes, and gain confidence in their abilities.

By regularly engaging in feedback and coaching, leaders instill a culture of continuous improvement within their teams. This culture encourages an open exchange of ideas, fosters innovation, and promotes a proactive approach to professional development. It transforms the workplace into a dynamic learning environment where everyone is committed to advancing not only their own skills but also contributing to the team's success.

Adopting an instructor's mindset to provide feedback and coaching is a powerful strategy for any leader. It not only enhances individual and team performance but also builds a supportive atmosphere which encourages ongoing personal and professional development. Leaders who excel in these areas are not just managing a team; they are equipping their team members with the tools and confidence to navigate their paths successfully, much like an instructor ensures a student pilot is prepared for solo flights and beyond.

6. Reflecting and Adapting:

Reflective leadership, much like effective instruction, involves a continuous cycle of assessment, adaptation, and enhancement. Leaders who embody this practice not only maintain the efficacy of their strategies but also foster a culture of growth and resilience within their teams.

The best leaders, similar to the most effective instructors, regularly reflect on their performance. This reflective practice involves critically assessing various aspects of their leadership—from

decision-making and team management to communication and conflict resolution. By taking the time to evaluate what's working and what isn't, leaders can pinpoint areas that require change or improvement.

Adaptation is a critical component of reflective leadership. Based on their reflections, effective leaders are willing to modify their approaches and strategies to better meet the needs of their teams and the demands of the environment. This might mean altering communication styles to enhance clarity, reshaping team structures to improve efficiency, or adopting new technologies to increase productivity. Adaptation ensures leadership methods stay relevant and effective, even as external conditions evolve.

By engaging in reflective practice and adaptation, leaders not only enhance their own effectiveness but also model these critical behaviors for their team members. This modeling sets a powerful example, showing that continuous improvement is valued and expected. It encourages team members to also reflect on their performance and seek ways to improve, fostering a proactive and forward-thinking work culture.

Incorporating the principles of effective instruction into leadership transforms the workplace into a dynamic learning environment. Here, challenges are seen as opportunities for growth, mistakes are acknowledged as essential steps toward mastery, and every achievement adds to a collective journey toward excellence. This environment encourages team members to experiment, take calculated risks, and innovate, knowing the focus is on progression and learning, not just on outcomes.

As leaders embrace and integrate the roles of instructor and reflective practitioner, they pave the way for a future where learning and growth are at the core of the organizational ethos. This approach not only meets immediate goals but also ensures that the organization is well-prepared to adapt to future challenges. The commitment to continuous learning and adaptation becomes the driving force behind sustained innovation and success.

Reflective leadership—characterized by ongoing reflection and a willingness to adapt—is crucial for maintaining the relevance and effectiveness of leadership practices. Leaders who commit to this approach not only optimize their own performance but also inspire their teams to embrace a mindset of continuous improvement. This strategy not only enhances day-to-day operations but also ensures long-term organizational resilience and success.

Safe skies and tailwinds, always. Let's chat again soon.

Chapter 20

Navigating Through Turbulence: Leadership In Emergencies

Welcome back to our exploration of the vast and often unpredictable skies of leadership. Today, we focus on a critical aspect of leadership: navigating through unexpected turbulence and emergencies. Just as pilots are meticulously trained to handle crises with utmost calm and precision, leaders must also be prepared to steer their teams through turbulent times with confidence and composure.

Effective leadership during emergencies begins long before a crisis actually hits. Preparation is key.

Leaders, akin to pilots, must have a deep understanding of their 'aircraft'—the team, the organization's structure, and its operations. This knowledge, combined with well-prepared emergency procedures and contingency plans, equips leaders to act decisively and maintain calm when faced with sudden challenges.

This type of preparedness is engrained in pilots both military and civilian. So much so, many do not look forward to returning for simulator training as they know well before arriving the training will include bad weather, a few emergencies, and having to make quick judgment decisions based upon everything being completed during a short training window. Some would call these training sessions stepping out of the frying pan and into the fire.

In the midst of a crisis, leaders must act as the pilot in command— making critical decisions swiftly yet thoughtfully. They rely on pre-established emergency procedures which have been carefully crafted and rehearsed with the team. These procedures ensure everyone knows their role and responsibilities in times of crisis, which minimizes panic and enhances collective efficacy.

The ability to remain calm and collected during emergencies is a hallmark of both skilled pilots and exemplary leaders. This composure reassures the team, fosters a sense of security, and prevents the spread of chaos and fear. Leaders must communicate clearly and confidently and direct their teams with assurance, ensuring all actions are coordinated and effective.

Navigating through a crisis involves more than just initial responses; it requires ongoing adjustment and vigilance as the situation evolves. Leaders must continuously assess the effectiveness of their actions and make real-time adjustments as necessary. This dynamic response can be the difference between navigating safely through a storm and succumbing to it. Remember, someone has to remain at the controls of the aircraft.

After navigating through an emergency, effective leaders, much like pilots after a turbulent flight, engage in thorough debriefing sessions. These reflections are crucial for learning from the experience and improving future responses. What worked well? What could have been handled better? Answering these questions helps in refining crisis management strategies and prepares the team even better for future challenges.

Navigating through turbulence and emergencies demands that leaders blend preparation, calmness, strategic thinking, and adaptability. By mastering these skills, leaders can ensure they not only guide their teams through crises effectively but also emerge stronger and more cohesive. Just as pilots earn the trust of their passengers by navigating safely through storms, leaders earn the trust and respect of their teams by adeptly managing crises, thereby reinforcing their role as dependable stewards of their organizations.

Pre-Flight Preparation: Anticipating the Unexpected

Just as an experienced pilot meticulously prepares before every flight, effective leaders recognize the importance of preparation in successfully navigating potential crises. The ability to anticipate and prepare for the unexpected is a hallmark of proficient leadership, ensuring that when challenges arise, the response is both swift and sure.

Leaders, just like pilots, must immerse themselves in continuous learning and training. This involves not only understanding the current landscape of their industry but also staying informed about potential risks and innovations. By studying trends, market shifts, and new technologies, leaders can better anticipate future challenges and opportunities.

One effective strategy any leader can borrow from pilots is the simulation of crisis scenarios. Just as pilots use simulators to practice handling various emergencies, leaders can conduct scenario-based training exercises with their teams. These simulations can range from financial downturns to operational disruptions, allowing team members to practice their responses to different crises in a controlled, low-risk environment.

Preparation also involves developing comprehensive contingency plans that outline specific steps to be taken in response to possible emergencies. These plans should be regularly reviewed and updated to reflect new information and changing conditions. By having a well-

thought-out plan in place, leaders ensure the team is not caught completely off-guard and can respond effectively to unexpected situations.

Another critical aspect of preparation is empowering team members by providing them with the knowledge and tools they need to handle crises. This might involve specialized training, access to critical information, or delegating authority to make decisions in emergency situations. When team members feel empowered and capable, they are more likely to take initiative and act confidently under pressure.

Ultimately, effective pre-flight preparation also involves cultivating a resilient organizational culture which can withstand and adapt to unforeseen challenges. This culture is characterized by flexibility, open communication, and mutual support—qualities which enable organizations to respond dynamically to changes and bounce back stronger from setbacks.

Like thorough pre-flight preparations undertaken by pilots, anticipatory leadership involves meticulous planning, continuous training, and empowering team members. While thorough preflight preparation similar to a pilot's rigorous checks is essential, leaders must recognize it's impossible to anticipate every possible scenario. The dynamic nature of the world means even the most comprehensive plans may not cover every contingency. This inherent unpredictability underscores the importance of cultivating adaptability and resilience within the team.

Effective leaders invest in building flexible systems and fostering a culture where innovation and quick thinking are encouraged. By preparing teams not just to follow a fixed plan but to adapt intelligently to unforeseen circumstances, leaders can navigate through uncertainties more confidently. This approach not only enhances the team's readiness for unexpected challenges but also fortifies the organization's overall resilience, ensuring it can thrive even when faced with the unknown.

Leaders who excel in anticipating the unexpected not only safeguard their organizations against potential crises but also position them for success in a volatile world. This proactive approach not only enhances the team's readiness but also instills a sense of confidence and reliability which permeates throughout the organization.

Risk Assessment: A Proactive Approach to Leadership

In the realm of leadership, regularly reviewing operations and projects to identify and mitigate potential risks is crucial. This proactive approach ensures organizations can anticipate potential issues before they become problems, safeguarding resources, and maintaining project momentum.

Effective leaders understand that risk assessment is not a one-time task but a continuous process which needs to be integrated into the daily operations of the organization. By regularly evaluating potential risks, leaders can implement strategies to mitigate them early on, which helps in maintaining stability and reliability in operations. This ongoing process involves analyzing both internal and external factors which could impact the organization's objectives.

Adopting a structured approach to risk assessment typically involves several steps: identifying potential risks, analyzing their impact, prioritizing them based on their likelihood and potential damage, and developing strategies to address them. This might include diversifying resources, enhancing security measures, or developing contingency plans.

Nina Vaca, the founder, and CEO of Pinnacle Group, exemplifies effective risk assessment in leadership. As a Hispanic-American entrepreneur, Mrs. Vaca has navigated her company through various economic cycles by meticulously assessing risks and adapting her business strategies accordingly. Under her leadership, Pinnacle Group has not only survived but thrived, largely due to her proactive approach to risk management. Her ability to foresee industry trends and adjust her business model has been critical in Pinnacle's growth, demonstrating the power of integrating risk assessment into organizational leadership.

Beyond individual assessments, effective leaders foster a risk-aware culture within their organization. This involves training team members to recognize potential risks and encouraging them to communicate their observations. Such a culture promotes transparency and collective responsibility, enhancing the organization's overall ability to respond to challenges swiftly and effectively.

Risk assessment is a fundamental aspect of strategic leadership. Leaders who excel in this area, like Nina Vaca, not only protect their organizations from potential downsides but also position them to seize opportunities which others might miss due to unmitigated risks. Regularly engaging in risk assessment prepares organizations to handle unexpected challenges and paves the way for sustained success and stability.

Crisis Planning: Crafting Actionable Emergency Procedures

Effective crisis planning is a cornerstone of strong leadership, especially in today's fast-paced and unpredictable environment. Leaders who excel in crisis management understand the importance of developing clear, actionable emergency procedures tailored to various scenarios, ensuring their team can respond swiftly and efficiently when challenges arise.

Crisis planning involves more than just generic strategies; it requires specific, detailed action plans which are customized to address different potential emergencies. These plans include step-by-step instructions designed to help team members know exactly what to do and when reducing confusion and enabling a more coordinated response.

A structured approach to developing these plans typically involves identifying potential crises, assessing their likely impacts, and crafting procedures which mitigate risks while safeguarding critical assets and operations. This proactive planning allows organizations to maintain control during crises and minimize their impact on operations and reputation.

Rosalind Brewer, a prominent African American business executive, has demonstrated exceptional crisis management skills in her roles as COO of Starbucks and CEO of Walgreens. At Starbucks, Brewer was instrumental during the company's public relations crisis following a racial bias incident in 2018. She played a key role in steering the company through the aftermath by helping to establish and implement inclusive policies and training programs, which were crucial in rebuilding the company's image and trust with the public.

Her leadership was again tested and proven during her tenure at Walgreens amidst the COVID-19 pandemic. Brewer led the expansion of COVID-19 testing and vaccine distribution, adapting the company's operations to meet critical public health needs effectively. Her ability to quickly mobilize resources, collaborate with government agencies, and ensure the safety of staff and customers exemplified her strong crisis management capabilities.

Crisis planning is an essential skill for leaders aiming to safeguard their organizations and ensure their teams are prepared for any eventuality. Leaders who, like Rosalind Brewer, successfully managed significant crises, employing clear, actionable strategies to guide large organizations through challenging times and instill confidence among stakeholders and employees.

Training and Drills: Ensuring Preparedness in Crisis Situations

Effective crisis management is not only about having a plan but also ensuring everyone involved knows their role and can perform it under pressure. Conducting regular training sessions and drills is critical for preparing teams to handle emergencies efficiently and effectively. Regular training sessions serve multiple purposes. They not only reinforce the specific tasks and responsibilities each team member must perform during a crisis but also help to keep these procedures fresh in the minds of employees. This continual reinforcement is crucial for maintaining a high level of readiness and can make a significant difference in the effectiveness of the response when a crisis actually occurs.

Drills take training a step further by simulating crisis conditions, allowing team members to practice their roles in real-time scenarios. These simulations help to identify any weaknesses in the emergency plans and provide a practical, hands-on experience which can be invaluable during an actual crisis. Drills ensure theoretical knowledge is translated into effective action by providing a realistic context for teams to hone their skills.

Regular training and drills also enhance coordination among team members, fostering a sense of teamwork and communication that is essential during high-pressure situations. By working together in drills, team members learn to trust each other's abilities and understand better how their roles fit into the larger crisis response plan. This coordination is crucial for ensuring that the team functions as a cohesive unit during emergencies.

Another significant benefit of regular training and drills is the increase in confidence they build among team members. Knowing what to do and having practiced it multiple times reduces panic and anxiety, which can be detrimental in a crisis situation. Confident team members are more likely to respond calmly and efficiently, making effective decisions and taking appropriate actions.

Conducting regular training sessions and drills is indispensable for any organization taking crisis preparedness seriously. These activities ensure every team member knows their role and responsibilities and can perform them effectively under stress. Training and drills prepare teams not just to react to crises but to manage them in ways which minimize damage and maintain safety. By investing in regular training, leaders can ensure their teams are not only prepared to face crises but are also more resilient and capable in their everyday roles.

Parallel Applications: Army Aviation Training and Business World Preparedness

In Army Aviation, the emphasis on repetitive drills and continuous training exercises is integral to building a highly-skilled, responsive, and cohesive unit. These rigorous training protocols are designed not just to maintain proficiency but to ingrain a deep-rooted sense of preparedness which pervades every aspect of the unit's operations. The disciplined approach to training and drills provides valuable lessons for business leadership and crisis management. Much like military units, businesses can benefit significantly from implementing systematic training and regular drills to prepare for potential crises and enhance overall operational efficiency.

Continuous Skill Development

Repetitive training exercises in Army Aviation serve to ensure every pilot and crew member is thoroughly familiar with their aircraft and their role in both standard and emergency procedures. In the business world, continuous training exercises can be akin to professional development programs which keep employees up to date with the latest industry standards, technologies, and methodologies. Regular training sessions help ensure employees:

☞ **Stay Competent:** Maintain high levels of proficiency in their specific roles.

☞ **Adapt to Changes:** Quickly adapt to market or technological changes which impact their work.

☞ **Skill Retention:** Regular repetition helps to solidify the skills needed to operate complex aviation systems under various scenarios, ensuring that these skills become second nature.

☞ **Error Minimization:** Consistent practice reduces the likelihood of errors in actual operations, as crew members become adept at anticipating and correcting potential issues before they escalate.

☞ Scenario-Based Planning: Simulating crisis scenarios in a business context can involve roleplaying exercises or simulated emergencies to test the organization's response to unexpected financial, operational, or reputational challenges.

☞ These simulations serve to:

☞ **Enhance Problem-Solving Skills:** Employees can develop and refine their problem-solving and decision-making skills in a controlled, risk-free environment.

☞ **Identify System Weaknesses:** Help pinpoint vulnerabilities in the organization's strategies and processes, allowing for timely adjustments.

☞ **Test Readiness:** Simulations test the unit's ability to execute operations under pressure, providing a realistic sense of the chaos and urgency that can occur during actual combat or rescue missions.

☞ **Identify Weaknesses:** By creating conditions that push the limits of the crew's capabilities, leaders can identify areas where additional training is needed, ensuring continuous improvement.

☞ **Strengthening Team Collaboration:** Just as military drills enhance coordination and trust among crew members, regular collaborative exercises in a business setting can improve teamwork and communication across departments.

☞ These activities encourage employees to:

☞ **Work Cohesively:** Promote a culture of collaboration and mutual support, in crucial during high-pressure situations.

☞ **Build Trust:** Establish stronger interpersonal relationships, which facilitates other cooperation and communication.

☞ **Anticipate Each Other's Actions:** Frequent drilling allows team members to predict and seamlessly react to the actions of their peers, enhancing operational efficiency.

☞ **Develop Trust:** Trust is built on the assurance that each member is equally capable and committed to the mission, a sentiment fostered by observing each other's competence during repeated drills.

Building Confidence and Reducing Workplace Anxiety

Confidence built through repetitive practice of business processes and emergency procedures can reduce anxiety and improve overall workplace morale. Confident employees are more likely to:

☞ **Handle Stress Effectively:** Manage stress during peak business cycles or organizational changes.

☞ **Take Initiative:** Feel empowered to take initiative and lead projects or problem-solving efforts.

☞ **Reduces Panic:** In high-stakes environments, a confident team is less likely to panic and more likely to execute their training effectively.

☞ **Improves Decision-Making:** Confidence allows pilots and crew to make swift, informed decisions that could mean the difference between mission success and failure.

Integrating the military-inspired practices of regular drills and continuous training into business operations can significantly boost an organization's readiness and resilience. These practices not only prepare businesses to manage crises more effectively but also enhance day-to-day operations by improving efficiency, teamwork, and employee morale. By adopting a disciplined approach to training and crisis management, businesses can ensure that they are as prepared as Army Aviation units to tackle challenges head-on and maintain operational excellence.

In-Flight Tactics: Leading Through the Storm

When turbulence hits, the skill with which a pilot handles the aircraft can greatly influence the comfort and safety of everyone on board. Similarly, in leadership, navigating through organizational turbulence—be it economic downturns, internal crises, or external threats— requires a leader to respond with immediacy, confidence, and calm. This ability to maintain composure and clarity under pressure is crucial for safeguarding the team's trust and stability.

In both aviation and leadership, timely responses are critical. Just as a pilot must quickly adjust to sudden changes in flight conditions, a leader must swiftly address challenges as they arise. Delays in response can escalate issues, potentially leading to greater disruptions. Leaders must assess situations rapidly and act promptly to implement necessary measures that will stabilize the organization.

Confidence is contagious and particularly valuable in crisis situations. A pilot's confident handling of the aircraft reassures passengers, just as a leader's confident decision-making can instill a sense of security among team members. This confidence should be based on experience, knowledge, and preparedness, empowering leaders to make decisions that navigate the organization safely through rough patches.

Calmness under pressure helps to preserve clear thinking and effective leadership. A pilot must remain calm to operate the aircraft effectively, and similarly, leaders must manage their emotions to maintain clear judgment. By staying calm, leaders can better analyze situations, communicate effectively, and prevent panic from undermining team morale and effectiveness.

Just as a pilot communicates with passengers during turbulence to reassure them, leaders should communicate openly with their teams during crises. Transparency in sharing what is known, what is unknown, and what steps are being taken helps to build trust and maintain calm within the team. Effective communication can prevent misinformation and speculation from spreading, which is vital for maintaining collective focus and morale.

Mastering in-flight tactics in leadership involves more than just steering the team through a crisis; it requires an approach that combines immediate action, confident decision-making, and sustained calm. Leaders who excel in these areas reassure and inspire their teams, much like a skilled pilot maintains the trust and safety of their crew and passengers. By leading effectively through the storm, leaders not only overcome immediate challenges but also strengthen the resilience and cohesiveness of their teams for future challenges.

Clear Communication: The Lifeline of Effective Leadership

In the wide world of leadership, the ability to communicate clearly and effectively is paramount. Just as a pilot must keep open and accurate lines of communication with air traffic control, crew, and passengers, a leader must ensure information flows seamlessly across all levels of the organization. This clarity and precision in communication are critical for ensuring that all stakeholders are well-informed and aligned with the organization's goals and strategies.

Maintaining open lines of communication means information should be accessible to everyone who needs it, when they need it. Leaders must establish and uphold channels which promote easy and efficient exchange of information. This might involve regular team meetings, updated digital communication platforms, or structured reports which keep everyone in the loop.

The timeliness of communication is just as important as its openness. Information must be relayed promptly to allow team members and stakeholders to react or make decisions based on the most current data. Delays in disseminating information can lead to missed opportunities, redundancies, or even errors in execution. Effective leaders prioritize swift communication to enhance responsiveness and agility within the team.

Accuracy in communication ensures the information being shared is correct and unambiguous. This precision prevents misunderstandings and mistakes capable of derailing projects or leading to inefficiencies. Leaders must be meticulous in how information is presented, avoiding jargon or ambiguity which might confuse or mislead the recipient. Clarity helps in building trust and reliability, as stakeholders feel confident in the leader's messages and directives.

Consistency in communication reinforces understanding and trust. When messages are consistent, they reinforce the organization's values and objectives, helping to keep everyone aligned and focused. Inconsistent messaging, on the other hand, can create confusion and diminish trust in leadership. Leaders must ensure their communications, whether verbal, written, or digital, consistently reflect the organization's standards and goals.

Clear communication is not just a supplementary skill for leaders; it is a strategic imperative that underpins every aspect of effective leadership. By ensuring that communication lines are open, prompt, accurate, and consistent, leaders can effectively coordinate efforts, align their teams, manage stakeholders, and steer the organization toward success. Clear communication acts as the lifeline that connects various parts of the organization, enabling smooth operations and fostering a culture of transparency and collaboration.

Visibility: The Cornerstone of Effective Leadership

In leadership, visibility is much more than just being seen; it's about being actively present and engaged with your team. A leader's visible presence, especially during challenging times, acts as a stabilizing force, providing reassurance and demonstrating the control and confidence needed to guide the team through uncertainty.

A leader's physical and emotional presence can greatly influence team morale. Being visibly engaged with team members' activities and challenges communicates that leadership is attentive and committed to their well-being and success. This reassurance is particularly crucial in times of stress or change, where uncertainty can lead to anxiety and disruption among the team.

Visibility also involves demonstrating control over the situation and exuding confidence in the face of challenges. When leaders handle situations with composure and decisiveness, it instills a sense of confidence in the team, reassuring them they are in capable hands. This doesn't mean leaders should appear infallible but rather they are proactive in addressing issues and confident in their approach to solutions.

General Ann E. Dunwoody, the first woman to achieve a four-star officer rank in the U.S. military, exemplifies the impact of leader visibility. Throughout her career, General Dunwoody was known for her hands-on leadership style. She frequently visited troops in the field, demonstrating control and providing direct support, which not only boosted morale but also reinforced her commitment to her soldiers' success and wellbeing. Her visibility, especially in operational environments, underscored her leadership capabilities and fostered a deep sense of trust and respect among her troops. I personally witnessed the impacts of simply showing up meant to all cohorts of the military apparatus.

Regular and meaningful interactions between leaders and their teams build trust over time. Trust is foundational in any relationship, particularly in the workplace where collaboration and mutual reliance are key to achieving goals. A leader who is consistently visible and accessible is more likely to foster a strong bond of trust, as team members feel supported and valued.

A visible leader enhances communication channels within the team. By regularly interacting with team members, leaders can gather insights directly from the frontline, understand the challenges being faced, and provide immediate feedback or support. This open line of communication ensures issues are addressed promptly, and team members feel heard and respected.

Leader visibility is a strategic asset in any organization. It goes beyond mere physical presence to encompass emotional support, open communication, and active engagement with the team. Being a visible, reassuring presence, leaders not only stabilize team morale, but they enhance overall productivity and cohesion. This approach to leadership not only helps navigate the team through immediate challenges but also builds a robust foundation for long-term success, ensuring the team feels continuously supported and motivated.

Being a visible, reassuring presence, and demonstrating control and confidence that can help stabilize the team's morale.

Decisiveness: Making swift, informed decisions based on the best available information, even when under pressure.

Post-Emergency Debrief: Learning from the Experience

After safely navigating through an emergency, pilots and their crews conduct a thorough debrief to review what happened, what was done well, and what could be improved. This practice is invaluable for leaders as well. It presents an opportunity to:

Analyze the Response: Examine the effectiveness of the crisis response and identify any gaps or areas for improvement.

Strengthen Team Cohesion: Acknowledge the team's efforts and resilience, reinforcing bonds strengthened through shared adversity.

Incorporate Lessons Learned: Update emergency procedures and plans based on insights gained, ensuring better preparedness for future challenges.

Here are a few examples of Leadership in Emergencies:

☞ **Chesley "Sully" Sullenberger's Hudson River Landing:** When US Airways Flight 1549 struck a flock of geese and lost engine power, Captain Sully's calm demeanor and decisive action saved the lives of all 155 people on board. His ability to remain composed under pressure and execute an emergency water landing exemplifies leadership in crisis.

☞ **Sheryl Sandberg and Facebook's Privacy Crisis:** During Facebook's privacy and data misuse scandals, COO Sheryl Sandberg faced intense scrutiny and pressure.

Her approach to navigating the crisis, focusing on open communication, taking responsibility, and implementing changes, demonstrated leadership resilience and the ability to restore trust in times of turmoil.

The Calm in the Eye of the Storm

Leadership, much like piloting, requires the ability to remain calm and focused in the face of emergencies, guiding your team with confidence and clarity. By preparing in advance, acting decisively during the crisis, and learning from the experience, leaders can navigate even the most turbulent skies and emerge stronger on the other side.

As we continue our journey through the leadership skies, remember that turbulence and emergencies, while challenging, also offer opportunities for growth, learning, and strengthening team bonds. Just as a skilled pilot uses their training and judgment to bring passengers safely through the storm, so too can effective leaders guide their teams through crises to clear skies and calmer waters ahead. Safe skies and tailwinds, always.

Chapter 21

The Quiet Altitude: Reflections From The Leadership Flight Deck

In the high-flying journey of leadership, amidst the bustling terminals of decision-making and the turbulent skies of daily challenges, lies an oftenoverlooked sanctuary: the quiet altitude of reflection. It's here, in the rarefied air of solitude and thought, that leaders find the clarity, perspective, and wisdom to navigate their courses more effectively. This chapter delves into the crucial practice of taking time for reflection, illustrating its importance with examples of renowned leaders who have embraced this practice.

The Importance of Reflective Leadership

Reflection, in the context of leadership, is the deliberate pause taken to contemplate, analyze, and learn from one's experiences. It's a time to step back from the operational controls, to survey the horizon, and to consider the broader landscape of one's leadership journey. This practice is not merely a luxury; it's a necessity for any leader aiming to cultivate a deeper understanding of themselves, their team, and their mission.

Examples of Reflective Leaders

Steve Jobs: The co-founder of Apple was known for his reflective retreats, particularly his long walks, which he used as opportunities for deep thought and contemplation. Jobs believed that walking facilitated creativity and problem-solving.

This practice was instrumental in some of Apple's most innovative products, showcasing how reflection can lead to groundbreaking ideas and solutions.

Bill Gates: The Microsoft co-founder takes what he calls "Think Weeks" twice a year, secluding himself in a cabin to do nothing but read and think. This tradition has been a part of Gates's routine for decades, allowing him time away from the day-today operations of his company to focus on learning, innovation, and future planning.

Winston Churchill: The former British Prime Minister and Nobel laureate was an advocate of what he called "pondering time." Churchill's reflective periods were spent painting, bricklaying, or simply sitting quietly. He believed these activities allowed him to detach and thus return to his duties with a refreshed perspective and renewed vigor.

Incorporating Reflection into Leadership Practice

Reflective leadership can take many forms, depending on individual preferences and circumstances. Here are some ways leaders can integrate reflection into their routines:

Scheduled Reflection Time: Set aside regular intervals—be it daily, weekly, or monthly—for reflection. This could be a quiet hour in the morning, a walk during lunch, or a weekend retreat.

Reflective Journaling: Keeping a leadership journal provides a space to record thoughts, challenges, successes, and lessons learned. Over time, this journal becomes a valuable resource for growth and self-awareness.

Meditation and Mindfulness: Practices like meditation and mindfulness can help clear the mental clutter, fostering a state of presence and focus that is conducive to reflection.

Strategic Retreats: Like Bill Gates's Think Weeks, taking extended time away from the daily grind can provide the space needed for deep strategic thinking and innovation.

The Outcomes of Reflection

The practice of reflection yields numerous benefits, including improved decision-making, increased creativity, greater emotional intelligence, and enhanced leadership effectiveness. By taking the time to reflect, leaders can develop a more profound understanding of their actions and their impacts, learn from their experiences, and approach their roles with greater wisdom and insight.

The View from Above

Reflection offers leaders a view from above, a chance to see beyond the immediate turbulence to the broader landscape of their leadership journey. It's in these moments of quiet contemplation that leaders can reconnect with their core values, reassess their goals, and chart a course that is true to their vision and mission.

Just as a pilot must occasionally break through the clouds to find clear skies, so too must leaders ascend to the quiet altitude of reflection to find clarity and direction. In doing so, they not only enhance their capacity to lead but also embark on a journey of continuous personal and professional growth.

To leadership, to learning, and to the limitless skies that await. Don't give up, the beginning is always the hardest.

Conclusion

The Journey Continues

As we conclude this book, let us remember that the journey of leadership is never truly complete. Each day brings new challenges to overcome, new lessons to learn, and new horizons to explore. The skies of leadership are vast and filled with limitless potential. It is up to us, as leaders and instructors, to embrace this journey with courage, curiosity, and a commitment to excellence.

Thank you for joining me on this voyage through the leadership skies. May your journey be marked by clear visions, steady growth, and a lasting impact on those you lead. Here's to the adventures that await, the challenges that will shape us, and the legacies we will build.

The journey continues, and the skies are calling. Let's soar to new heights together. As we chart our course into the endless expanse of leadership skies, let's carry with us the lessons learned and the insights gained. Leadership, in its truest form, is a voyage of discovery, not just of external landscapes but of the internal terrains of our hearts and minds.

"It's not about perfect. It's about effort. And when you bring that effort every single day, that's where transformation happens. That's how change occurs."

- Jillian Michaels

Embarking on New Journeys

The end of this book is not an ending but a beginning— a launchpad for new journeys, new challenges, and new opportunities to make a difference. As leaders, our mission is to inspire, guide, and empower, but also to remain students of the vast and ever-changing world around us. Let us embrace the unknown with enthusiasm, for it is in the unknown that the greatest opportunities for growth lie.

Fostering Innovation and Creativity

The skies of leadership are boundless, offering infinite possibilities for innovation and creativity. Encourage your team to dream big, to question the status quo, and to imagine what could be. By fostering an environment where new ideas are celebrated and explored, we not only drive progress within our organizations but also contribute to the broader evolution of our industries and communities.

The Legacy of Leadership

What legacy will you leave as a leader? This question, more than any other, should guide our actions and decisions. Leadership is not measured by the heights we reach alone but by the extent to which we lift others along the way. Let us strive to leave a legacy of kindness, integrity, and excellence—a legacy that inspires the next generation to reach even greater heights.

In contemplating the legacy, we wish to leave, consider the enduring principles of the wolf pack. Just as the Alpha Wolf ensures the safety, unity, and progression of the pack, so too should we aim to foster a culture of mutual support, resilience, and collective success within our teams. Leadership is about more than individual achievements; it's about the impact we have on others and the foundations we lay for future leaders. By embodying the wolf pack mentality, where every role is respected and every contribution valued, we can inspire and uplift those around us, paving the way for a legacy that, like the paths through the wilderness, guides and protects long after our tenure. Let this be the measure of our leadership—a legacy that, through kindness, integrity, and excellence, empowers others to ascend to new heights and continue the journey forward.

A Call to Action

As this book closes, consider it a call to action. The principles and practices explored within these pages are but a compass—tools to guide you on your leadership journey. The true test lies in the application of these lessons in the real world, in the daily acts of leadership that shape our lives and the lives of those we lead.

> *"If you can't fly then run, if you can't run then walk, if you can't walk then crawl, but whatever you do you have to keep moving forward."*

-Martin Luther King Jr.

Gratitude and Reflection

In closing, I offer my heartfelt gratitude to you, the reader, for embarking on this journey with me. Reflect on the path we've traveled together, the lessons learned, and the insights gained. May they serve as beacons of light, guiding you through the challenges and opportunities that lie ahead.

The Horizon Awaits

As we part ways, remember that the horizon always beckons with new adventures, new challenges, and new opportunities to make a difference. The journey of leadership is eternal, ever-evolving, and infinitely rewarding.

So, here's to the journey ahead, to the leaders we will become, and to the impact we will make. The skies are wide open, the horizon awaits, and the best of our leadership journey lies just beyond the next cloud.

JOEL D. SMITH
STRATEGIC LEADERSHIP ADVISOR   INTERNATIONAL SPEAKER   EXECUTIVE COACH
LEARN HOW WE CAN ELEVATE YOUR TEAM'S PERFORMANCE AT:
WWW.THEJOELSMITH.COM

LEAD FROM HERE

9 798330 366958